Satwant Singh is a nurse consultant... Therapy (CBT) and mental health... Improving Access to Psychological Therapies (IAPT) service. Satwant has been working in the field of CBT since 1994 and specifically working with individuals with issues of hoarding since 1998. He has been facilitating the UK's only treatment group – the monthly London Hoarding Treatment group – since 2005. Satwant is involved in a number of research projects, some in the area of hoarding, with King's College London and with his colleague Dr Colin Jones. He has been actively involved in teaching and training in CBT both nationally and internationally. Satwant regularly presents at conferences and facilitates workshops in CBT and hoarding disorders.

Margaret Hooper is a cognitive behavioural therapist and counselling psychologist. Margaret has a special interest in hoarding and has been involved in co-facilitating the London Hoarding Treatment group alongside Satwant since 2005. She has worked as a CBT therapist since 2005 and works in the NHS in an NHS specialist CBT service for individuals with long-term health conditions.

Colin Jones is a senior lecturer and researcher in advanced clinical practice at a large UK university. He has a special interest in life history, reminiscence and narrative research methods and is a member scholar of the International Institute of Qualitative Methodology, Canada. Colin has been involved in numerous research projects in Japan, south-east Asia, Europe and the UK, most recently within the area of hoarding. Together with colleague Satwant Singh, he is further developing photo-elicitation methods designed specifically for hoarding research, in which photographs are used as a tool to explore and develop an understanding about individuals, telling a story about their situation.

The aim of the **Overcoming** series is to enable people with a range of common problems and disorders to take control of their own recovery programme.

Each title, with its specially tailored programme, is devised by a practising clinician using the latest techniques of Cognitive Behavioural Therapy – techniques which have been shown to be highly effective in changing the way patients think about themselves and their problems.

Many books in the Overcoming series are recommended by the UK Department of Health under the Books on Prescription scheme.

OVERCOMING HOARDING

A self-help guide to using
Cognitive Behavioural Techniques

Satwant Singh,
Margaret Hooper
and
Colin Jones

ROBINSON

ROBINSON

First published in Great Britain in 2015 by Robinson

Copyright © Satwant Singh, Margaret Hooper, Colin Jones, 2015

5 7 9 10 8 6 4

The moral rights of the authors have been asserted.

Important Note
This book is not intended as a substitute for medical advice or treatment.
Any person with a condition requiring medical attention should consult a
qualified medical practitioner or suitable therapist.

A CIP catalogue record for this book
is available from the British Library.

ISBN: 978-1-47212-005-2

Typeset in Bembo by Initial Typesetting Services, Edinburgh

Printed and bound by CPI Group (UK) Ltd, Croydon, CR0 4YY

Papers used by Robinson are from well-managed forests
and other responsible sources

Robinson
An imprint of
Little, Brown Book Group
Carmelite House
50 Victoria Embankment
London EC4Y 0DZ

An Hachette UK Company
www.hachette.co.uk

www.improvementzone.co.uk

This book is dedicated to all the participants of the London Hoarding Treatment group. They have acknowledged their issues, faced their challenges and helped develop our treatment programme. Without their courage, work and support this book would not have been a possibility.

Why a cognitive behavioural approach?

The approach this book takes in attempting to help you overcome your problems with hoarding is a 'cognitive behavioural' one. A brief account of the history of this form of intervention might be useful and encouraging. In the 1950s and '60s a set of therapeutic techniques was developed, collectively termed 'behaviour therapy'. These techniques shared two basic features. First, they aimed to remove symptoms (such as anxiety) by dealing with those symptoms themselves, rather than their deep-seated underlying historical causes (traditionally the focus of psychoanalysis, the approach developed by Sigmund Freud and his associates). Second, they were scientifically based, in the sense that they used techniques derived from what laboratory psychologists were finding out about the mechanisms of learning, and they put these techniques to scientific test. The area where behaviour therapy initially proved to be of most value was in the treatment of anxiety disorders, especially specific phobias (such as extreme fear of animals or heights) and agoraphobia, both notoriously difficult to treat using conventional psychotherapies.

After an initial flush of enthusiasm, discontent with behaviour therapy grew. There were a number of reasons for this. An important concern was the fact that behaviour therapy did not deal with the internal thoughts that were so obviously central to the distress that many patients were experiencing. In particular, behaviour therapy proved inadequate when it came to the treatment of depression. In the late 1960s and early 1970s a treatment for depression was developed called 'cognitive therapy'. The pioneer in this enterprise was an American psychiatrist, Professor Aaron T. Beck. He developed a theory of depression which emphasized the importance of people's depressed styles of thinking, and, on the basis of this theory, he specified a new form of therapy. It would not be an exaggeration to say that Beck's work has changed the nature of psychotherapy, not just for depression but for a range of psychological problems.

The techniques introduced by Beck have been merged with the techniques developed earlier by the behaviour therapists to produce a therapeutic approach which has come to be known as 'cognitive behavioural therapy' (or CBT). This therapy has been subjected to the strictest scientific testing and has been found to be highly successful for a significant proportion of cases of depression. However, it has now become clear that specific patterns of disturbed thinking are associated with a wide range of psychological problems, not just depression, and that the treatments which deal with these are highly effective. So, effective cognitive behavioural treatments have been developed for a range of anxiety disorders, such as panic disorder, Generalised

Anxiety Disorder, specific phobias, social phobia, obsessive compulsive disorders, and hypochondriasis (health anxiety), as well as for other conditions such as drug addictions, and eating disorders like bulimia nervosa. Indeed, cognitive behavioural techniques have been found to have an application beyond the narrow categories of psychological disorders. They have been applied effectively, for example, to helping people with low self-esteem, those with weight problems, couples with marital difficulties, as well as those who wish to give up smoking or deal with drinking problems. The current self-help manual is concerned with hoarding. Until recently, people who hoarded objects in a manner that was distressing and disabling were regarded as having a form of psychological dysfunction known as 'obsessive-compulsive disorder'. However, it has come to be recognized that hoarding has rather particular characteristics and, as such, should be considered as a problem in its own right. The current manual provides a detailed analysis of the nature of hoarding and the difficulties it causes, together with specific techniques for overcoming hoarding and the associated problems people experience.

The starting point for CBT is the realisation that the way we think, feel and behave are all intimately linked, and changing the way we think about ourselves, our experiences and the world around us changes the way we feel and what we are able to do. So, for example, by helping a depressed person identify and challenge their automatic depressive thoughts, a route out of the cycle of depressive thoughts and feelings can be found. Similarly, habitual behavioural responses are driven by a complex set of thoughts and feelings; and CBT, as you will discover from this book, by providing a means for the behaviour, thoughts and feelings to be brought under control, enables these responses to be undermined and a different kind of life to be possible.

Although effective CBT treatments have been developed for a wide range of disorders and problems, these treatments are not widely available; and, when people try on their own to help themselves, they often, inadvertently, do things which make matters worse. Over the past two decades, the community of cognitive behavioural therapists has responded to this situation. What they have done is to take the principles and techniques of specific cognitive behavioural therapies for particular problems, of proven effectiveness, and present them in manuals which people can read and apply themselves. These manuals specify a systematic programme of treatment which the person works through to overcome their difficulties. In this way, cognitive behavioural therapeutic techniques of established value are being made available on the widest possible basis.

The use of self-help manuals is never going to replace the need for therapists. Many people with emotional and behavioural problems will need the help of a trained therapist. It is also the case that, despite the widespread success of cognitive behavioural therapy, some people will not respond to it and will need one of the other treatments available. Nevertheless, although research on the use of these self-help manuals is at an early stage, the work done to date indicates that for a great many people such a manual is sufficient for them to overcome their problems without professional help. Sadly, many people suffer on their own for years. Sometimes they feel reluctant to seek help without first making a serious effort to manage on their own. Sometimes they feel too awkward or even ashamed to ask for help. Sometimes appropriate help is not forthcoming despite their efforts to find it. For many of these people the cognitive behavioural self-help manual will provide a lifeline to a better future.

Professor Peter J. Cooper,
University of Reading, 2015

Acknowledgements

The authors would like to extend their appreciation and thanks to Paul Perkins for his time, reviews and helpful feedback and to Mark S. Elliot for his illustrations. We also thank our colleagues and friends for their support and valuable feedback.

Contents

Part three

Part four

Hoarding

We are a special group of people
We keep many things
Not for us the bulging dustbins
Or recycling bins

Not for us the pristine houses
Everything shut away
We prefer to keep stuff near us
For another day

Piles and stacks and hoards of all sorts
Books and music, clothes and tins
All together we can see them
Boxes, bric-a-brac and things

Piled high a blaze of colour
All startling to the eyes
Stuff in bags and piles and boxes
Coloured piles of every size

Small bags, big bags or recycling
Bags are needed for the stuff
Black sacks, green sacks, cardboard boxes
We can never have enough

But these bags
They cause a problem
Where to walk and stand and sit
Move them over ever upward
Our living space is just a bit

We develop ways of walking
Like a crab upon a shore
Sideways, slow our feet are seeking
A small space upon the floor

Overcoming Hoarding

But I joke, it is not funny
In fact, it's much the opposite
Stuff we have and in abundance
But there's nowhere much to sit

Only we who have this problem
Realise that it's bad
We do not want our friends to see it
That is why it's sad

Shame and worry
And self-loathing
They all play a bit
Sitting in our choked up houses
Surveying all the shit

Yes, it is poetic licence
Yes, I shouldn't swear
And, yet it makes me feel so wretched
Whenever I am there

We do not choose to have this problem
For us it is so very sad
Like something there within our psyche
But it doesn't mean we're bad

Funny looks or threats from neighbours
Lead to acute embarrassment
We fear reports to health and safety
Will a summons to us be sent?

Even families can hurt us
When they grumble at our stuff
They think we're stupid, mad or lazy
They do not understand enough

Hoarding

Will we ever solve this problem?
Can a lasting cure be found?
Thanks to research from caring people
We may be slowly breaking ground

Slow but sure there is an answer
From this self-paralysis
We can do our best to help them
And tell them how it really is

R. S. H. – a participant of the
London Hoarding Treatment group

Introduction

Why did we write this book?

Hoarding is a common disorder that affects many people in one way or another. The authors of this book received countless enquiries from people suffering from hoarding issues but it was impossible for us to be able to offer treatment individually. In 2005 we set up the UK's only service for those with hoarding issues and their family and carers, an open group called the London Hoarding Treatment group.

Over the years people from all over the UK and abroad have attended the London group. We decided to write this book based upon our work to benefit those who are not able to access treatment and for those providing it. We have developed innovative ways of successfully engaging people using experiential methods in conjunction with the principles of Cognitive Behavioural Therapy (CBT). The participation of the London Hoarding Group members has been instrumental in the development of these innovative techniques. Over the years, their experiences and successes have informed us of the value in combining these methods to allow people to help themselves with their hoarding issues.

Using a self-help book cannot be a cure or quick fix for you in itself but it can be the first step in dealing with your problems and can enable you to identify the next stage of your journey towards reclaiming your space and your life. CBT itself is based on the self-help model with the aim of helping an individual to be his or her own therapist. On reflection, you will gain awareness about your capacity to deal with issues that may arise, while no single type of therapy is able to bring about change without your participation and willingness to engage in the process.

This book is aimed at helping you to recognise your ability to resolve and overcome your own difficulties and will help you apply this to deal with your hoarding issues.

Who is this book for?

This book has been written with the intention of helping and supporting:

The individual with hoarding issues.
Family, friends and carers.
Professionals who work with people with hoarding issues.

It is important to remember that it is never possible to meet the needs of everyone. However, this book is structured in a way that people using it will be able to adapt it to their individual requirements.

How is the book structured?

Our experience in running the group has enabled us to

appreciate the difficulties that people and their family, friends and carers encounter and we have attempted to design each chapter with your family, friends and carers' needs in mind.

Each chapter has been written with the aim of covering a specific area and can be used on its own as some sections may not apply to everybody. In each chapter you can expect an introduction, the steps to follow, guided exercises, obstacles you may encounter, tips, information for family and friends to help support you and a summary of the key messages of the chapter.

The book is divided into four parts. Part one discusses general information about hoarding. This will describe hoarding disorder, how we can understand it and how it impacts you, your family, friends and the environment in which you live. This section will also address some of the environmental health issues that surround hoarding and the consequences that individuals with severe hoarding issues may experience.

Part two looks at the interventions that you can use yourself. These interventions are those we have found useful and developed with the participants of our group programme. Each and every individual is unique and some interventions suggested in the book may bring their own challenges. We will also attempt to highlight some of these challenges and address ways of overcoming them.

Part three identifies ways in which you can start re-engaging with life. It is important to note that this process is a key feature throughout the book. You do not have to wait until you get to this point in the text. Indeed, recognising that you have a problem means that you have already taken the first step on the journey to reclaiming your space and your life.

Part four discusses ways of maintaining your progress, identifying traps and developing a plan to prevent relapse. This is an important area to focus upon. It is normal to have periods where progress slips, leading to feelings of discouragement and even making you want to give up. We find it more helpful not to see these times as relapses but rather as setbacks which may even have opportunities. Planning will help you deal with these occasions and keep you focused on aspects that are important to you. Each setback provides you with a chance to be creative, focus on your resilience and develop new strategies for coping. Each and every one of us has survived life having to face challenges on a daily basis. Dealing with these challenges often goes without notice and is taken for granted. Human beings have an inner resilience that has enabled us to reach our present stage in life. This book is also designed to help you recognise your resilience, your progress and your capacity to change in dealing with difficulties.

Next steps

Having read this section and come this far, if you have any questions or concerns that come to mind, it is worth taking the time to write them down. As you work through this book, hopefully these questions will be answered. These questions will also help you identify potential obstacles that you may face in overcoming your hoarding issues. This will be helpful in part two of the book when we are discussing interventions.

Part one

Hoarding Disorder

What is hoarding disorder?

People with hoarding disorder save and collect things to excess and find it very difficult to get rid of items. They often have a cluttered living space at home or elsewhere and experience distress and find it hard to function fully within their personal or work environment when it no longer functions for its intended purpose. For example, a bedroom may not be useable for sleeping or a kitchen may not have space in which to prepare and cook meals.

Hoarding becomes a problem when it starts affecting the ability of a person to live in the comfort and safety of their own home. Additionally, clutter becomes a health and safety issue not only to them, but also to those living with them and their neighbours. Fire poses the greatest risk, followed by the possibility of infestation by vermin. Injuries from tripping and falls are common and, in the extreme, people have been reported to have died after being buried under their clutter.

Often people become very distressed when they come under the scrutiny of statutory authorities such as environmental health, housing departments and emergency services. Officials view excessive clutter as something with the potential to endanger the hoarder and this can lead to prosecution. Furthermore, legal action can result in an individual's home being forcefully cleared and increases emotional distress, stigmatisation and discrimination.

DSM-5

The *Diagnostic and Statistical Manual 5* (*DSM-5*), published by the American Psychiatric Association, has a category for hoarding disorder or compulsive hoarding, as it was formally known. *DSM-5* is a standard guide for therapists and recognition for hoarding means it is likely that further research will be carried out. As it has been categorised as a specific disorder, treatment can be developed to target hoarding and outcomes can be evaluated.

To be diagnosed with hoarding disorder, the individual has to meet the following five criteria:

1. Persistent difficulty discarding or parting with possessions which may be perceived as useless or of limited value as a result of strong urges to save items. Distress may be experienced and/or difficulty in making decisions associated with discarding.

2. Hoarding symptoms manifest themselves in the collection and accumulation of a large number of possessions. These clutter the active living areas of the home, workplace, or other personal environment and prevent the use of the space for its intended purpose.

3. The symptoms of hoarding cause significant distress or impairment for an individual in social, occupational or other functional areas.

4. The symptoms are not a result of a general medical condition.

5. The symptoms are not a result of another psychological condition.

Who is affected by hoarding disorder?

Hoarding can affect anyone. It does not discriminate in terms of occupation, education status, religion, gender, sexual orientation or age. Hoarding disorder does not only have an impact on the individual who shows the symptoms but also on their family members, carers and friends. Often sufferers do not allow family or friends to visit their home. When family members share living space with those affected they can find it extremely difficult to cope with the restricted environment and the reaction to moving or handling items that have been hoarded.

Why do people hoard?

There is no single reason why people hoard. Research has shown that experiencing some form of traumatic event can contribute towards hoarding behaviour. Others use hoarding behaviours as a way of coping with emotional distress.

For some, it may be strong emotional and sentimental attachment of values to objects.

Some people have strong beliefs about the value of knowledge and tend to hoard related materials such as books, magazines and newspapers. For others, hoarding can be a learned behaviour. Perhaps they have grown up in an environment where items were saved and the significance of keeping and not wasting things was considered vitally important. This could play a part in the development of the disorder.

Other factors that may contribute to the problem include ingrained perfectionistic tendencies, high standards, difficulty making decisions, need for control, strong beliefs about the significance of items saved and also deprivation – those who may have once been denied objects can hoard as a way of compensating. Moreover, a lack of significant personal relationships can lead to the development of an attachment to objects as a replacement. For these people, the objects represent stability, remaining a constant feature in their environment and life. Saved items may provide a link to positive memories and good times, so they help create an environment of safety and comfort.

How common is hoarding disorder?

Hoarding disorder is a common condition but because many people feel embarrassment and shame about it, exact figures about its prevalence are difficult to obtain. In reality, almost everyone has hoarding traits but these may not manifest as a problem. It is estimated that between 4–6 per cent of the population have difficulties with the condition and the number of people accessing help has increased with recent media attention as more sufferers are beginning to recognise that they may have a problem. Many others only realise that they have a hoarding problem when their homes require maintenance or when they receive complaints from neighbours or visits from housing support teams, family and friends or the emergency services.

What objects make up a hoard?

Anything and everything can be hoarded. As each person is individual so are the items they choose to hang on to. Common objects include clothes, photographs, crockery, furniture and even animals. A hoard tends to have some personal significance, value or perceived usefulness although, in extreme cases, people keep apparently bizarre items such as faeces and urine – but even these will have personal relevance.

Items can have direct or indirect significance. Direct significance might be ascribed to an item bought or acquired in person, perhaps received as a gift or inherited. Indirect significance can be tied to an object by association and has no direct link to the individual. A concert programme can be collected as a reminder or memory of someone having mentioned the event.

Where do people hoard?

The home is the most common environment for a hoard, although they can be found anywhere that a person with the disorder has access. Garages, storage facilities and offices can be used. Often, friends and family are implicated in hoarding behaviours by providing the temporary relief of additional storage space, resulting in their own environment becoming cluttered.

Impact of hoarding on the individual, others and environment

Hoarding disorder impacts the individual on many different levels. Firstly, the environment is cluttered, leaving no comfortable space or room. Secondly, personal relationships are affected. Thirdly, the ability to engage in normal activities is disrupted. Finally, feelings of shame, anxiety and fear of a stigmatised perception by others often leads to social isolation.

Those living within the same environment often exhibit similarly high levels of stress and anxiety as the individual with hoarding issues who controls the space in which they live. Their movements within their home are restricted; they have no personal space for themselves due to the clutter. Often family members report considerable anger within the environment. The resulting tension can cause a deterioration of relationships.

Friends are often not allowed to visit for fear that they may judge the person who hoards. Over time, the individual's personal relationships and friendships deteriorate to the point where they end up living alone and isolated.

Clutter prevents maintenance from being undertaken due to the inaccessibility of areas that need repair and the reluctance of workers to enter affected premises. In the long term this often leads to further damage. Many sufferers live without heating or hot water when the boiler breaks down and they cannot get a repair carried out. As a result, they rely on other means of heating, such as bar or blow heaters, which can themselves present a further hazard as they can cause fires by igniting the clutter. The risk of fire also affects others living within the home, neighbours and the property itself. The hoarding of food also poses a danger through vermin infestation.

People with hoarding disorder are particularly vulnerable to environmental health laws. These are in place to protect the population at large and to ensure that they are able to live within a community that is safe and minimises the potential for harm.

Individuals with hoarding behaviours are also subject to civil laws if they are seen as being a nuisance to society. In the UK, there have been a number of people who have been issued with anti-social behaviour orders (ASBOs), which are restrictive and punitive considering that they suffer from a psychological condition.

What do we know from research?

Recent research has shown that hoarding is a disorder in its own right. Encouragingly, this work also shows that treatment is effective for those who engage in therapy and are motivated to change. Over the years, therapy has developed and improved to target hoarding beliefs and behaviours.

Other health conditions

As with any psychological condition, it is possible that those suffering from hoarding disorder can also have other conditions. Depression and anxiety are the most common problems, while other conditions include obsessive-compulsive disorder (OCD), attention deficit hyperactivity disorder (ADHD), eating disorders, post-traumatic stress disorder (PTSD), bereavement disorder and adjustment disorders (difficulty in coming to terms with changes in circumstances such as the ending of a relationship, employment changes or moving house). These additional issues can interfere with the treatment of the hoarding disorder. For example, if an individual is suffering from depression, the impact of the depression can affect their ability and desire to engage in dealing with their hoarding issues. In addition to mental health issues, people may also suffer from physical health problems that can compound their difficulties.

Treatment for hoarding disorder

The early research undertaken into the treatment of hoarding disorder offered treatment based on the CBT treatment protocol for OCD. This was a result of the fact that most individuals with hoarding disorder seeking help were also showing signs of OCD. The outcome of these studies was poor and participants did not make much improvement. Treatment did not specifically target the hoarding disorder as it was assumed that hoarding was a symptom of OCD. Therefore it was difficult to identify which specific condition was being treated.

However, over the last few years, outcome studies have concentrated on providing therapy and treatment based on the CBT model for hoarding disorder. The results of these studies have been more favourable. These therapies range from individual to group, web-based to consulting room-based and include some home-based sessions. Studies have demonstrated that for treatment to be effective there needs to be a mixture of consulting room and home-based sessions.

Medication for hoarding disorder

Research has concluded that medication is not helpful in the treatment of hoarding disorder. However, those people with other conditions such as depression and anxiety may find that medication may be of benefit in improving their mood and reducing their anxiety levels, which will enable them to engage better in dealing with their hoarding issues. Medication is best discussed with a doctor or psychiatrist. If you are affected by these issues and are taking medication, it is important to take it as prescribed and, if you have any concerns or worries, you should consult your doctor.

Stopping medication without prior discussion with your doctor is not advisable.

Key messages

- Hoarding is characterised by the excessive collection of things, saving and difficulty in discarding.
- Hoarding is now recognised as a disorder.
- Hoarding affects sufferers and their family and friends on many levels.
- Hoarding can cause an individual to be socially isolated.
- Almost everyone has hoarding tendencies and the disorder affects 4–6 per cent of the population.
- There is no single reason why people hoard.
- People hoard anything and everything that is significant to them.
- People with hoarding issues can experience other psychological difficulties such as depression and OCD.
- Research has shown that CBT is an effective treatment for hoarding disorder.
- Medication can help other comorbid (simultaneously present) psychological difficulties.
- Legislative environmental health laws can be enforced to have homes cleared for the protection of others and maintenance of the building.

How do I know if
I have a problem?

A question that people often ask is, 'How do I know if I have a problem?' It is a perfectly legitimate one, as recognising and accepting that one has a problem is not easy at all. There have been a host of recent television programmes on the subject and even dedicated hoarding disorder cable channels. These have had both a positive impact in terms of instilling hope that help is available and a negative influence in demonstrating that the condition can be stigmatising.

The media provides information and raises awareness of the condition but it also explores the shame associated with the disorder in many programmes. The key message should be that hoarding affects each individual in different ways. The label or diagnosis is less significant than the ways in which the condition affects a person in terms of their ability to live their life fully.

But if almost everyone has hoarding or saving traits and we all tend to save things that are significant to us, how can we tell that we have a problem? You can ask yourself questions that may help to identify how far you are along the spectrum:

Do you find it difficult to walk in your environment without knocking over items, walking sideways, having to walk with your back against the wall?

Does the number of possessions in your environment result in it not being used as intended? For example, does the clutter on your bed make it difficult to sleep, does the kitchen lack space to cook and does the living room require rearranging to be usable?

Do you avoid inviting your family and friends home?

Do you buy things that you do not use and instead save them?

Do you collect multiple copies of the same item?

Do you find it difficult finding things in your home, such as documents, clothes and books?

Do you find it difficult to discard things without a lengthy checking procedure?

Do you find that you spend too much time worrying or thinking before discarding something?

Do you feel distress or discomfort when you have to throw things away?

Do you spend a lot of time making a decision before discarding things?

Do you find it difficult giving things away?

Do you find it difficult utilising the things you own, such as clothes?

Do you keep things even though you longer use them, for example clothes that are too small or big, or empty containers?

Do you find that after you have thrown things away, you have gone and collected them back from the bins?

Do you find that you cannot trust your mind in remembering things?

If you find that you have answered five or more of the above questions with a 'Yes' then you should ask yourself: 'Is my space and life affected by the amount of things that I have?' If so, you may have a hoarding problem. You may find it useful to ask a family member or friend that you trust for their opinion or view. Do *they* consider that you have a hoarding issue?

It can be difficult for us to distinguish whether or not we have excessive belongings in our space. We become familiar with our living environment and it becomes the norm for us. Sometimes we can talk ourselves into thinking that we are OK and do not have a problem – we may reassure ourselves that our clutter is temporary and we will sort it out when there is more storage space or when we give things away.

What is therapy?

Therapy, in its simplest form, can be defined as the treatment of psychological difficulties. In our experience, anything that gives you some comfort is a form of therapy. For example, talking to a friend about a stressful situation can be a form of therapy. Therapy does not have to be formal.

Self-help is informal therapy. Self-help is about healing and getting back on track by using our own resources. Each and every one of us can tap into these to deal with our issues. In this book, the terms 'therapy' and 'treatment' will be used interchangeably and have the same meaning.

We have written this book in a way that places you in the driving seat on the journey to being your own helper or therapist. You have control of the pace and the amount of time you wish to invest in helping yourself with your hoarding issues.

Often, we can all feel that we are not able to deal with issues when they arise as we feel overwhelmed. This book allows you, as the reader, the space to step back to have a breather before continuing. If you reflect over the course of your lifetime, you will probably see that you have been dealing with and are continuing to deal with your challenges as they arise. Sometimes you may not recognise how you have coped with or negotiated the difficulties you have encountered in life. The time has come to start a journey by recognising that you are taking the first step in reclaiming your space and regaining your life.

Therapy

There are many different types of therapy that suit different problems. The treatment strategies in this book are based on Cognitive Behavioural Therapy (CBT), a form of talking therapy. This is one of the most researched treatments and the clinical outcomes have demonstrated that it is highly effective for a range of psychological problems.

In its most basic form, CBT works with the ways our beliefs and thoughts affect the way we feel and react to situations, an example of which is illustrated on p. 22.

We can see from the illustration that the way we view or interpret a situation can affect the way we feel and react to it. CBT responds to this by addressing the three components of any daily task: thought, emotion and behaviour. Through CBT we are encouraged to take steps to intervene in our difficulties. This book will focus on all three components of CBT work. Exercises will cover each aspect and, while reading a book will not on its own bring about any changes, putting the theory into practice should help the process of change. It is like watching a cookery programme; to be able to enjoy the dish on the TV you must first be prepared to try making it. Your meal may not turn out the way you want at the first attempt, but with practise it

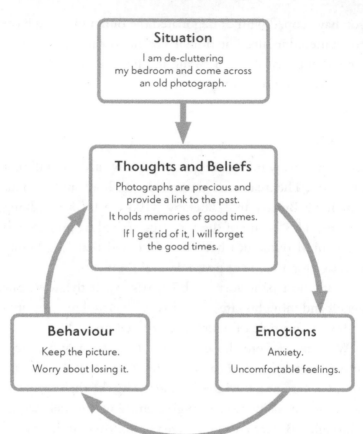

Situation

I am de-cluttering
my bedroom and come across
an old photograph.

Thoughts and Beliefs

Photographs are precious and
provide a link to the past.

It holds memories of good times.

If I get rid of it, I will forget
the good times.

Behaviour

Keep the picture.
Worry about losing it.

Emotions

Anxiety.
Uncomfortable feelings.

will get better. Therapy works very much along the same principles. In CBT it is important to work on the exercises and as you carry them out it will become easier for you. You will develop skills in dealing with your problem and the progress you make will motivate you further.

As with any other type of therapy, CBT helps you to develop knowledge of your difficulties. You learn to identify triggers, understand how your problem keeps going and how to practice helpful interventions. You may never know all the reasons why you hoard, but CBT can give you a start in overcoming the disorder in a practical sense. It is important to remember that you cannot change the past, but instead you can focus on the present and how you would like the future to be – a future in which you deal with your clutter and hoarding to reclaim your space and your life.

What does the work in this book involve?

We will help you identify your vision of how you would like your living space and your life to be. Then the following stages will address your motivation and understanding of your problem and give you step–by–step exercises to help deal with your hoarding issues and their consequences. It is important to remember that you have ownership of your problems and you are accountable only to yourself. No one can force you to do what you do not wish to do. When you have doubts or difficulties, we have found that it is useful to go back to your initial vision to help you make the choices to deal with your problems.

The exercises in this book have been designed based on the work we have undertaken with the London Hoarding Treatment group. We have tried to uncover potential difficulties and provide solutions based on our experiences of working with the group. As each person is individual and unique, so are your problems. We will not be able to cover all potential problems but we can give you the underlying principles. This is what self-help is about, so take a moment to consider the situations that you are faced with on a daily basis. You will find that you apply your skills and knowledge all the time and you can adapt and transfer those skills to deal with other issues as they arise.

It is important to remember that undertaking the exercises will help you with your problem as they will enable you to master the challenges you face. The exercises have been designed to target the key issues that people with hoarding disorder present.

Living our lives is time-consuming and things that are important to us, such as our self-care, can take second or third place or be neglected altogether. It is important to make sure that your journey to reclaiming your space and your life is a high priority.

Part of our self-care is ensuring that we live in an environment that provides us with safety and comfort. Sometimes, when we do not value our space as part of our self-care, we can find ourselves hoarding. As part of the process of overcoming your issues, you may need to reconsider your priorities so that you can work effectively in dealing with your clutter.

Having read this far about CBT, you are now on the road to becoming your own therapist. In part two, you will start to address your hoarding issues. Remember to go one step at a time, working systematically and consistently. The next chapter will address some of the basics, which are important to understand before you start the exercises.

Key messages

- Therapy is the treatment for psychological difficulties.
- Anyone can be their own therapist.
- Plan your therapy to fit in with your schedule.
- CBT is one of the most researched talking therapies and has good clinical outcomes.
- CBT is focused on our thoughts, feelings and behaviours.
- CBT is based on the self-help model and has tasks and exercises to help develop your skills in dealing with your issues.
- Having an understanding of your problem is the first step to recovery.
- The journey of reclaiming your space and life will involve undertaking the exercises to build on your current skills.

Family and friends

The consequences of hoarding can be far-reaching for those close to a sufferer and in this chapter we look at what you can do if you are a friend or a family member of someone with hoarding disorder.

There may be practical difficulties gaining access to parts of the home or there may be health and safety concerns. Financial issues may include the cost of acquiring multiple copies of one item or indeed things that are not required. It may result in the non-payment of bills and incur fines, in some cases due to the inability to locate necessary papers or letters. There is also the distress caused by feeling unable to help or being frustrated when the best of intentions don't seem to make a difference or even make things worse.

Hoarding places a strain on relationships when loved ones do not recognise that they have a hoarding problem. Family and friends may also, unknowingly, perpetuate the condition by following the wishes of the person who hoards too closely – for example, by giving up their own space in a wardrobe or a shelf to accommodate more of their possessions. Yet as someone close to the individual with hoarding behaviour, you need to ensure you do not get into a blaming mode that will damage your relationship. It is not always easy to strike a balance between being sympathetic and firm – but it is necessary.

What can you do as a friend or family member?

You may have tried in many ways to help your friend or family member to understand the problems that their hoarding causes, but these may not have had any impact or may even have made things harder. If what you are doing is not working you can consider other choices. One option can be to leave them information about hoarding, such as a leaflet, information from the internet, a book or a DVD. The person who is hoarding may pick it up in your absence and read it out of curiosity.

You can also gather more information yourself. You may be able to attend a support or treatment group – with or without the person concerned. This can help you to understand more fully the condition and the ways to deal with it.

Given that the hoarding is likely to have been going on for many years, it may take time for the person who is hoarding to acknowledge that things have now got out of hand and that changes are needed. Your role is to facilitate change and help them to start to deal with their problem by providing support, motivation and encouragement. However, avoid the temptation to try and clear up on your own. Without the person's permission, this well-meaning move is likely to worsen the problem and cause further emotional distress. The responsibility for the clearing lies with the person doing the hoarding.

Urgent action

You may need to take more direct action in certain cases. If the need to clear is urgent (for example, if there is a health and safety or legal issue), you should negotiate your role with your friend or family member in order to help more actively. Taking the time to talk before acting helps maintain trust and establishes roles.

How can I support my family member or friend?

Being there and being supportive while they start to clear can be really helpful. A good way to start is to encourage the person who is dealing with hoarding to target one area; you should encourage them to take photographs of the area before clearing it and ensure the items leave the home after the clearing session. Targeting a small area at a time ensures that the work takes place at your friend or family member's pace. You can also play a role in rewarding the clearing activity by spending time enjoying the space or going out together afterwards to do a pleasurable activity. Building trust and confidence as a helper is important. Sometimes another person who is dealing with their hoarding – perhaps a support worker or a volunteer – may also be able to help.

How can I develop my understanding about hoarding?

Gaining an insight into the difficulties yourself may help you to better support your friend or family member. Try to imagine that someone has thrown away one of your most treasured items and that you cannot retrieve it. Picture the thoughts that would run through your mind. Now try to put yourself in the shoes of someone who hoards. You can appreciate some of the range and intensity of emotions that they may experience on a daily basis.

The hoarding continuum

No attachment to possessions   Problematic attachment to possessions

Are you more towards one end or the other? You may not have your living space full of objects but do you, for example, hoard texts or emails? Most people fall somewhere between the extremes.

Looking after yourself

In order to help others we all need to look after ourselves. Supporting someone who is dealing with their hoarding can at times be distressing as well as rewarding. This may vary depending on your relationship with the person and how often you are in their environment. It will therefore help to look after yourself physically by maintaining a healthy diet, exercising regularly and getting enough sleep. It is also important to make sure you have time to do the necessary day-to-day things. You need to make sure you take part in pleasurable and fun activities and are able to share your own difficulties with others. You may need support to be an effective helper. Being kind to yourself in these ways will help you cope more effectively with any difficult feelings. We all experience both positive and negative thoughts. These thoughts can influence the way we feel and react to situations. It is helpful to notice if negative thinking about the problem is taking over. It is important to remember that, ultimately, you can only do the best you can, and that the responsibility for tackling the hoarding problem lies with the individual.

Sometimes the person who hoards may not be aware of how their hoarding problem is impacting on you. It can be useful to let them know how their hoarding issues are affecting you and how they may be able to help. Statements beginning with 'I' can be helpful here, such as, 'I am anxious that someone may trip over these piles,' or 'I have a problem inviting my friends over as there are no chairs to sit on.' While you may not change the situation with words, you can gradually raise awareness of the difficulties you face. It may also make you feel that you have done the best you can to let your friend or family member know the effects of their hoarding behaviours.

In summary: give information, be there to support the person who hoards, help those close to you to attend a group, understand their difficulties as far as you can, help reward the positive actions and look after yourself. Keeping up a positive spirit and maintaining your sense of humour can help too!

Throughout the book you will find smaller sections with information for those close to the person who hoards – look out for 'family and friends' boxes as you work your way through the book.

Part two

1

Introducing the basics

We will soon be beginning the exercises in overcoming hoarding but first take the time to read some basic guidelines that will form the foundation of your journey. As you progress through this book, you will build on the information in this chapter with the aim of developing your skills in dealing with your hoarding issues. This section has been written to tie in with the general approach you will find throughout your work with us.

Time

Time is precious. We have demands that often conflict with our needs and those of others. It is important to remember to make time for yourself and to look after yourself. It is not selfish to think about putting yourself first. We often put others first and do not consider our own personal needs and what is important for us.

Remember, the time you give yourself does not have to be huge. You can begin by allowing yourself half an hour each day to work on your issues. As you progress you will find that you may prefer to allow yourself more time. Making time for yourself will also help you to start managing your day better.

Strategies to help you make time

- Write down all the things that you do each day for a week.
- Draw up an activity schedule for all your routine activities, such as working, sleeping and shopping.
- Identify a period of time that you can commit to on a regular basis for dealing with your hoarding.
- Keep to the activity schedule, in the same way we always keep to our schedule to go to work. Keeping to the activity schedule will ensure that you will be consistent with doing your tasks.
- Make a record of each day you stick to your schedule. This helps to reinforce your work and will provide a positive reminder that you have made the time to deal with your issues.
- Be consistent in your approach and do what you have planned to do to help you to deal with your hoarding issues.

Obstacles

Obstacles are common. Look out for them as they in reality can be traps that prevent us from doing what we need to do:

- 'I am too tired.'
- 'I do not have the time.'
- 'There is too much to do.'

When you face an obstacle, ask yourself, How can this help

me deal with my problem? Break the obstacle into smaller tasks to make it more manageable.

'I do not have anyone to report to about what I have done.'

Tell a friend you are going to do an important job and that, without discussing the details, you will report back when you have completed the work. Being accountable to someone will motivate you to plan your time appropriately so that you can carry out the task you had planned to complete. We will look at likely obstacles as we come to each part of these guidelines.

Photograph your environment

Take photographs of your surroundings before you start to work on your disorder. It will be a record of how things looked before you began your journey. They can be an important way to record the progress you make and will be used as part of your self-help treatment.

Strategies for taking photographs

- Take the photographs from the perspective that covers the biggest area.
- Take weekly photographs of the area you are working on to monitor your progress.
- Take the photographs from the same location each time to ensure consistency and prevent you from distorting your progress.

Obstacles

'I'm concerned about having the photographs developed and some-one seeing them.'

Most cameras and smartphones take digital images that can be downloaded and stored on a computer or a disk. These images are yours and no one can forcefully ask to see them.

'Someone might see them.'

These photographs are yours and if you have them on your digital camera or smartphone you can control who has access to them.

'I do not have a computer or the knowledge to use a computer.'

Photographs can be stored on your camera or phone. If you have a friend that you trust you could ask them to help you move them to a computer.

'I do not want to look at them.'

It is understandable that initially you may not wish to look at the photographs, but do still take them – you do not have to look at them. In time, you may find that you would like to see what your environment looked like and compare the past and the present.

Identifying an area to work on

It is in our nature when clearing to move from one area to the next without completing the first area. But if you are going to truly deal with the clutter, you will need to identify an area and stick with it until it is completely cleared.

Strategies for identifying an area to start on

Locate an area that is important to you to begin with – your bedroom could be one as it is important for you to have a clear bed to sleep on. Your kitchen is important for being able to cook. Now select a section within that area that you are going to work on. Work consistently in this section before moving on to another area. Resist the temptation to start somewhere else. Remain focused on this one small section. By maintaining your focus on this area, you will find that you will notice the difference as space increases and this will, in turn, motivate you to keep working on your hoarding issues.

Obstacles

'I am finding that as I work on the identified area, I keep doing other things or move to another area instead.'

There may be a number of reasons for this; it may appear to be too difficult, you may feel overwhelmed or unable to cope or maybe other areas appear to be easier or more interesting. To deal with this obstacle, keep your clearing session short and focused. Plan to do it before doing something pleasurable or fun. Step back and review what you have achieved so far.

'I am not doing enough, my room will never be clear of all the things I have in there.'

Recognise that you are working in one area in a systematic way, and you are gradually going to work on the whole area. Think of it as if you are doing a jigsaw puzzle and slowly but surely the puzzle will be complete.

Keep a record of how much you have done

It is always helpful to keep a record of what you have thrown out. The detail of what has been discarded is not important but the quantity can be. For example, how many bags have you used? How much space has been cleared?

It is normal to have good and bad days; on bad days it is often easy to feel despondent. When you feel this way, you tend to forget what you have achieved so far. Keeping a record will remind you how much you have done and how far you have come.

Strategy for keeping a record

Keep a record on a daily basis. Do not leave it until the next day – you will forget how much you have done and doubt yourself.

Obstacles

'I can't be bothered to write it down.'

Instead of writing, take photographs of the bags that you are going to throw away. Keeping a record does not have to be a complex task. Another easy way to record what you have been able to do on any one day is to mark the number of bags thrown out on your activity schedule or just on a calendar.

Be creative. You can use coloured dots, each colour representing a specific number of items. A black dot could represent one bag or a red dot could be five bags of material that have been thrown out.

Stay with the feeling

Undertaking activities that are not part of your normal routine could make you feel uncomfortable and anxious. Learn to acknowledge the discomfort and move on and the feeling itself will simply pass. The more we react against uncomfortable emotions, the stronger they get. By trying to get rid of the feeling you are only making it seem more significant. By letting feelings be – even uncomfortable ones – they will pass and you will be able to recognise your ability to cope with difficult emotions.

Strategies for staying with uncomfortable feelings

Recognise and accept what you are sensing. Accept it as it is normal to feel uncomfortable and anxious while you are doing things that you would not normally do. Be in the moment and engage in whatever you are doing. Stop thinking about your thoughts and questioning your feelings and be part of what is happening around you. Put on some music or the television in the background, or have a friend be with you while you are sorting and clearing things out.

Obstacles

'It is too uncomfortable. I can't cope with it.'

41

Accept the way you are feeling. Do not fight it and it will pass. The more you try to get rid of it, the more significant it becomes. Recall and recognise the other times when you have felt like this and survived.

'It will never go away.'

The more you engage with the feeling, the longer it will last. By having a dialogue with the feeling, you are making it more pronounced and it will become more uncomfortable. Think of the times when it has been hot and there was nothing you could do about it and how, over time, you tolerated the heat.

Seek support

It can be helpful to elicit support from family and friends. Sometimes just being aware that you have family and friends you can talk to may be adequate. Sometimes, having their physical presence when you are dealing with your clutter can be of great value. Family and friends can provide support in many different ways, from providing emotional support to actually physically helping with getting rid of things.

Strategies for seeking support and help

Speak to your family and friends and let them know what you would like from them. Let them know what support you need and how you would like them to provide that for you. Be clear and set some ground rules that would make it easier for you. It could be, 'I just need you to be with me, not doing any of the clearing,' or 'I need you to help me take these bags to the tip or to the charity shop' and so on.

Obstacles

'They will judge me.'

People commonly fear that others will judge them for the fact that their home is cluttered and untidy. In our experience, friends and family have usually been supportive when people have explained their situation.

'I feel shame.'

Shame is another common emotion. Remind yourself that you have not done anything wrong but are just trying to sort out your home and your life. People understand that sometimes others have problems. The fact you recognise that you have a problem and you are dealing with it is a commendable act and people are likely to respect you for being honest and dealing with a difficult problem.

'They will get rid of my things without my involvement.'

Explain to your friends or family what it is that you want them to do. Usually people do respect what you ask of them.

Putting things into practice

This book will introduce new ways of dealing with your hoarding issues. Some of the exercises will involve you doing things differently and the process can feel unfamiliar and threatening. Sometimes we forget that we are constantly dealing with issues on a daily basis and at times do them differently. Reflect on your activities and identify situations where you have had to deal with things differently and recognise how you have coped.

Strategy for putting things into practice

Take the risk. Taking risks is healthy and will help you to make changes that you feel are necessary. We learn from our experiences.

Obstacles

'I do not feel I can do it; it is not something I have done before.'

Do not allow your emotions to rule what you can or can't do. Instead, go through the experience of trying, as trying is the only way you can make an informed decision. Ask yourself about some of the things that you do now. Have they come from experiences? Look at how your experience of trying something new can help you to learn and deal with your issues.

'It feels too threatening.'

Ask yourself, What is threatening? How is it threatening? Is it just the idea of trying something new or different? Ask yourself, What is the worst that could happen?

Be creative

Sometimes things do not work out as planned. When that

is the case, be creative and substitute something else. Be flexible. Nothing is set in stone in this book. Each exercise is a guide. If you find you cannot carry it out as we have suggested, improvise something similar.

Strategies for being creative

There are many ways to do each task. There is no right or wrong way. Each of us has preferences and we like doing things in a certain way. Be bold, be creative and try doing each exercise differently, in a way that is not familiar.

Obstacles

'I usually put my things in a black bag before I take them out. I have run out of black bags.'

Use carrier bags instead, it makes no difference. Bags are just containers. The colour or type of bag makes little difference.

'I can only work on my clothes.'

Don't be fixated by one category. Expand your range – in this example by looking at something similar to clothes. Try instead to work on your towels or sheets instead of your clothes.

Celebrate each inch of space that you regain

Recognise and celebrate the space you regain and each activity you engage in. It is not easy, but start by seeing the colour in your home. The clutter has blocked out the light, the floor, walls and furnishing leaving your home dark and dull.

Strategies to recognise and celebrate what you have achieved

When you finish working on an area, look at it, stand in it, feel it and celebrate what you have achieved. It may be uncomfortable at first as the space may feel empty, but recognise what you have got back. Invite family and friends in and show them what you have done. Mark the area with something colourful. Look at the photographs that you took before and compare to how it is now. Print them if you can and see the difference.

Obstacles

'I have not done enough. It is too slow.'

Remind yourself that it has taken a period of time for your home to become cluttered and it will take time to get it back to where you want it. You take small steps in the beginning. As you get more confident, you will be able to deal with larger spaces and work through them. An inch is better than nothing.

Write notes of what works

As you work through this book, make a note of the exercises you undertake that you find helpful. You may wish to revisit them when you are faced with a difficult declutter. This will help you to maintain the good work you have undertaken and to develop the relapse prevention plan outlined in part four.

Strategies for taking notes

Write about your exercise as soon as you have completed it. Make a note of what was helpful. Be specific in identifying key interventions of the greatest value. Repeat the exercise if you can and apply it to other areas of your hoarding issues.

Obstacles

'I cannot remember.'

Do not rely on memory. Can you remember exactly what you did yesterday? Most of us struggle. You will find that trying to remember everything is not that easy. Making notes on a notepad will help you to recall the key points when you come back to your exercises.

'I do not have the time.'

Make the time. It only takes a couple of minutes to write it down. It is for your benefit and not for anyone else's.

'I have the book so I can always look at it.'

Yes, you have the book, but you may not always refer to it as often as you would like to. Take stock of all the books you have and ask yourself, How often have I consulted them?

These are some of the components of your journey that you will need to consider. These basics are important as they will help you work in a systematic way to deal with your hoarding issues. Reading through the basic principles in this chapter will help you to deal with some of the obstacles that you will experience on the route to reclaiming your space and your life.

2

Vision

Many self-help books set a goal or target and you may feel pressured into attaining this mark. In our experience, the term 'goal' is not very helpful. Instead, we have decided to use 'vision'.

Vision starts with a feeling that can be developed through your imagination. Creating a mental image is a powerful motivating force as it can evoke thoughts and emotions and so influence our behaviour and our reactions. Having such a guiding vision can be helpful in bringing about change. For example, consider the times when you have been out shopping for clothes. How often have you had an image in your mind of the style you want, the colour and the fit? This vision of what we are looking for helps us to make a decision about what we want.

Often, having lived in an environment that has been cluttered for a period of time, you lose the sense of what the space used to be. When clutter takes over, people often remark on the dullness and the lack of colour in addition to the inaccessibility of their belongings.

So let's start by developing your vision. Creating an image is a good start; it gives an idea of how you would like your environment to appear. If you have difficulty accessing an image, remember what the space used to look like. Look at photographs, pictures in magazines or draw a picture of how you would like your room to be. Write about your image and describe it in as much detail as you can. For example: My vision is to have a space where I can move about freely, even with my eyes closed. I will not bump into anything and fall over. I can see the colour of the walls and floor.

My vision is:

....

....

....

....

....

....

....

....

What next?

Think about your vision and your space. Select a room in your home that is, at this moment, significant to you. Ask yourself, How would I like this room to look? Describe in detail what that room would look like, including colour, items of furniture and space.

My vision is:

....

....

....

....

....

....

....

....

Now that you have this image and vision, ask yourself, What does it feel like?

....

....

....

....

....

....

....

....

Ask yourself, In which part of my body do I feel this feeling?

....

....

....

....

....

....

....

....

Place your hand where you feel this feeling, engage with it and ask yourself, What does this feeling mean to me?

....

....

....

....

....

....

....

....

Write down the steps that you need to maintain this feeling:
What do I need to do?

....

....

....

....

....

....

....

....

....

....

....

....

....

....

....

....

....

Now that we have a vision for your space, let's try to create a vision for your life. Imagine that you no longer have a cluttered environment and think about it. What would my life be like? What would I be doing differently? Who would be there?

....

....

....

....

....

....

....

What does it feel like?

....

....

....

....

....

....

....

Where do I feel this feeling in my body?

....

....

....

....

....

....

....

....

Place your hand where you feel this feeling, link to it and ask yourself, What does this feeling mean to me?

....

....

....

....

....

....

....

....

Write down all the steps that you need to maintain this feeling: What do I need to do?

....

....

....

....

....

....

....

....

....

....

....

....

....

....

....

....

....

Family and friends

It is important to look forward with a positive attitude. If the person with hoarding issues is happy to share their vision of a particular room or area, it can be helpful to reinforce that by reminding them of the good images and feelings. This is likely to be more beneficial than repeatedly talking about goals in a way that may just place pressure on your family member or friend. The way we express our future aims can suggest forward movement and act as a reward for useful action. Talk about how the space will be used, how you can contribute to the vision of the room and how you can share in their plans. You can provide a new perspective by having these discussions in a different space, perhaps a park or café. Supportive language is likely to result in better relationships and outcomes.

Tips

- Try developing your vision in a neutral environment such as a café, library, in your family or at a friend's home. Sometimes being away from your clutter can be helpful.
- Do you find it hard to create a vision? Use photographs, pictures in magazines and other found materials.
- Spend time with family and friends and discuss their lives. What steps do they take to achieve their own

goals? Draw on what they say to identify whether there is anything similar for you.

- Do not be over-ambitious. Start with a small vision that is achievable and that you can work towards. Visions can be flexible and can change.
- Be creative. Do not feel that there is only one way to deal with things, as there are many ways to do a task.
- Reinforce your vision by revisiting this exercise regularly.

Obstacles

'I can't imagine what I would like my home to be like.'

Look at pictures in magazines of homes. What do they look like? Visit a friend's home and observe how it is different from your home. What does it feel like to be in another environment?

'I can't imagine a different life.'

Try doing something different each day. For example, take a new route to work or talk to people. What is it like? Make a daily change and see what is possible. We can take small steps to make our way the way we want it to be. Small changes have a large impact.

'There is no one who can support me.'

Try to imagine that you are helping someone else. Imagine your present difficulty to be another person's and ask yourself, What would I say to this person? What steps can this person take? Apply these responses to your vision to help it become stronger.

Key messages

- Having a vision is a foundation for helping you reclaim your space and your life.
- Images and photographs are useful and powerful in helping create your vision.
- Using photographs is a good way to measure change.
- Engage with your feelings; they are important and can be motivating.
- Family and friends can be a good resource to help you.
- Taking small risks each day creates the possibility of doing things differently.
- Revisit your vision regularly to help you keep focused.

3

Motivation

Having identified your vision, you can now develop your motivation to make those important changes to your life. It can be difficult at times but, as ever, you take those small steps along the way. Those of us who have been trying to deal with our hoarding issues can find we feel so overwhelmed that we want to give up and it's important to feel the process is manageable. There are a number of tools that we can use as motivational aids.

H.O.A.R.D. acronym tool

With the help of our London treatment group we developed the H.O.A.R.D. acronym tool[1]. This has been designed to help you get started in dealing with your clutter. Before using it, you must first take photographs of your environment. As previously discussed, photographs and images are powerful tools. They can evoke memories, emotions and reactions that can help in unpacking experiences and feelings. From here you can start creating action points.

---

1 Singh, S. & Jones, C. (2012). 'Visual Research Methods: A novel approach to understanding the experiences of compulsive hoarders.' *Journal of Cognitive and Behavioural Psychotherapy Research*, 1 (1): 36-42.

H.O.A.R.D. works in conjunction with photographs to tell your story and this will help you to understand your problem and the impact it has on your life. In the next few chapters, we will work on helping you to develop this understanding and, along the way, hopefully answer some of your questions.

Using H.O.A.R.D

Step 1

In the basics chapter, we talked about taking photographs as part of your self-help. These photographs are an important aspect of your journey to reclaim your space and your life. They form a record and also act as a monitoring tool. Using the photographs of your environment, you can answer the five questions that make up H.O.A.R.D – and we'll come to those in a moment.

Firstly, it's important to choose a neutral environment. Take a selection of photographs to the neutral environment away from your hoarding to help you maintain an emotional distance from your problem. Having time away from our environment enables us to see the real situation with clarity. This insight enables us to start considering how our cluttered space could be different and what steps we can take to get there. The neutral spot could be anywhere such as a café, library, family or friend's home, or the park. You simply need to have privacy and time to use the tool.

Now go through the images that you have brought with you and select the one that is most important or stands out the most to you at this moment. The photograph you have chosen may be the room that you feel you need to work on most. Giving yourself time, study the photograph carefully and when you are ready answer the following five questions. Write in as much detail as you can.

H   **What has HAPPENED in this picture?**

O   **What would I like to OVERCOME and what are my goals?**

A   **Can I imagine life without ALL of this stuff?**

R   **How are my life and RELATIONSHIPS affected by this problem?**

D   **What would I like to DO about it?**

Once you have written down the answers, look at the photograph again and read your responses to the questions.

What has Happened in this picture – H.O.A.R.D.?

....

....

....

....

....

....

....

....

What would I like to Overcome and what are my goals – H.O.A.R.D.?

....

....

....

....

....

....

....

....

Can I imagine life without All this stuff – H.O.A.R.D.?

....

....

....

....

....

....

....

....

How are my life and Relationships affected by this problem – H.O.A.R.D.?

....

....

....

....

....

....

....

....

What would I like to Do about it – H.O.A.R.D.?

....

....

....

....

....

....

....

....

Look again at the photograph and your written responses. Focus on the **D** and write down each step that you need to take to deal with your hoarding issues. The steps that I need to take to deal with my hoarding issues are:

....

....

....

....

....

....

....

....

....

....

....

....

....

....

....

....

....

....

....

....

Imagery

Using imagery is another powerful tool to bring into play alongside H.O.A.R.D. Images hold emotions and these feelings can help motivate us to do things differently. As before, it is best that this exercise be carried out in a neutral environment. Read the instructions – in a moment you will need to close your eyes. You might want to ask a member of your family or a friend to help you by writing down your responses to each question.

Bring an image to your mind of how you would like the room you have identified to look. For example, you may have a mental picture of your furniture fully cleared of clutter or of a visible floor. Describe each aspect, including the furniture, floor, carpet, curtains or blinds. Notice how it feels as you see this.

Now close your eyes. Bring your image back into your mind. Hold that image and make a link with your original feeling. Ask yourself the following questions, writing the answers in as much detail as you can.

When I have the image of how I would like my space to look, what does it feel like?

....

....

....

....

....

....

....

....

....

....

Where do I feel this feeling in my body?

....

....

....

....

....

....

....

....

What does this feeling mean? What does it say about me?

....

....

....

....

....

....

....

....

In order to sustain this feeling, what do I need to do?

....

....

....

....

....

....

....

....

Cost/benefit analysis

When we engage in any activity or behaviour there are always costs and benefits that it can be helpful to weigh up. For example, suppose you are going to run in a race and need to practise. If you do not feel like doing your training run one day you have an immediate benefit – you get to stay at home. The cost will come on race day when you won't be as physically fit as you could be. Let's see how we can use that to affect hoarding issues.

To begin with, identify the behaviour you wish to work on, such as holding on to items. List all the costs and benefits to you and others in the short term and in the long term.

The behaviour I am analysing:

....

....

....

....

....

....

....

....

Short term benefits

For myself   **For others**

....
....
....
....
....
....
....
....
....
....
....
....
....
....
....
....

Long term benefits

For myself   **For others**

....

....

....

....

....

....

....

....

....

....

....

....

....

....

....

....

Short term costs

For myself   **For others**

....
....
....
....
....
....
....
....
....
....
....
....
....
....
....
....

Long term costs

For myself   **For others**

....

....

....

....

....

....

....

....

....

....

....

....

....

....

....

....

....

Now having listed both the costs and benefits of your chosen behaviour for yourself and others in the short and long term, review them and develop your action plan.

The behaviour I have analysed:

....

....

....

....

....

....

....

My plan to deal with my hoarding issues:

....

....

....

....

....

....

....

....

....

....

....

....

....

....

Family and friends

It is important to try to understand the level of support your friend or family member would value and asking appropriate questions can be one way of doing just that. If you've read the suggestions above, you might like to show that you are supporting them in taking photographs, in creating images and in feeling the positive emotions associated with their vision.

Let them decide how they wish to be supported and adapt to their needs. This could include calling or texting them, giving them space to look at their photos in your home or providing a reward after an exercise, such as an outing to a café or park. You could lend them a camera or phone, offer to write down their responses to H.O.A.R.D. questions, make a note of their imagery or write up their cost/benefit analysis exercises. You could also simply just be there for them.

Tips

- When working on your motivation to deal with your hoarding issues, it is beneficial to work in a neutral environment away from your home.
- Get in touch with your feelings; acknowledge and respect them. Emotions are powerful motivators. Recreate positive emotions frequently as they will help with sustaining your motivation.
- Use these positive emotions to help you stay focused.
- Whenever you feel like avoiding dealing with your hoarding issues, ask yourself, What are the costs and benefits of my avoidance?

Obstacles

'I do not have a camera to take the photographs.'

If you do not have a digital camera, use your mobile phone. Most mobile phones have a camera built in.

'I am embarrassed that someone will see the photographs.'

It is natural you would feel embarrassed should someone see your photographs. Find a neutral place that is not crowded to provide you with privacy and pick a time that is less busy if you are considering a public place such as a café. Or use the home of someone you know – having them around can be supportive.

'I can't choose the best photograph.'

The rule of thumb would be to consider the room that is most significant to you at this moment. Choose the room in which reclaiming that space would make your life the most comfortable at this time.

Key messages

- Motivation is an important element to sustain your journey to reclaim your space and your life.
- There are many ways to develop and sustain your motivation. Be creative and take risks. There is no right or wrong way.
- Family and friends can provide support and motivate you to do these exercises.
- In every action or behaviour there are costs and benefits.

4

Scheduling

Most people have a routine that they normally stick to. For example, if you are employed, you have a routine of getting up at a certain time, ensuring that you have a certain amount of time to get ready and travel to work. At work, we have a routine for how we engage with our duties. We stop around a specific time for our lunch break and so forth. In this chapter we will look at ways you can incorporate de-cluttering into your daily routine.

One way of developing a routine for your hoarding issues is to ensure that a specific time of day is devoted to dealing with your clutter. Having a routine will ensure consistency and your clearing will become a normal part of life rather than being a special effort. Routines also help us normalise our work around the problem and instil hope as we become aware that we are dealing with our clutter on a daily basis.

How do you start developing a routine?

To begin with it may be helpful to use an activity scheduling form, similar in style to a timetable. This has cells for each waking hour of the day in which you can record your activities. This will help you develop an understanding of how your time is spent and you can get a better idea of how you might tailor your activity to your lifestyle. Additionally, writing activities hourly will build an accurate record of your progress. It is easy to discount the milestones we have attained as we may consider them insignificant. It does not matter what you do, but making a permanent note of it will be helpful. Recording your activities will also help you with your beliefs, which we will discuss in a later chapter in this book.

How to identify your activities and plan your time

An easy way to record your activities is to use the activity scheduling chart on pages 82 and 83. The days have been divided into hourly segments. Do not feel that all the activities that you undertake have to be within those hourly segments. They can overlap. For example, let's say you went out shopping from 9.30 a.m. until 11.45 a.m. You can use half of each box. There may be times when you are not doing anything and you should make a note of your free time. Accurate recording will help you to make time to deal with your hoarding problem and clutter.

If you find that the activity schedule in this book does not suit your purposes, be creative and develop your own. You might find a larger piece of paper works better, particularly if you need to write more detail.

Highlight some of the areas that are core to your daily routine. These are things that cannot change, such as your working hours, college, etc. You may choose a different coloured pen for your commitments. It will help with distinguishing the activities that are flexible to change to a different time.

Family and friends

You may be able to help by providing a reminder to record activities on the schedule. You can also assist by suggesting ways to fit clearing into a daily routine based on the timetable or by adapting the existing routines to work better. If the schedule itself does not suit the person you are supporting, then be creative in generating new ways of recording the information. If the person is willing to share their clearing plans with you, don't interrupt or suggest activities at these times, unless it is to support the clearing itself.

Overcoming Hoarding

	Monday	Tuesday	Wednesday	Thursday	Friday	Saturday	Sunday
07.00–08.00							
08.00–09.00							
09.00–10.00							
10.00–11.00							
11.00–12.00							
12.00–13.00							
13.00–14.00							
14.00–15.00							

15.00–16.00	16.00–17.00	17.00–18.00	18.00–19.00	19.00–20.00	20.00–21.00	21.00–22.00	22.00–23.00	23.00–24.00

Tips

- We do daily tasks automatically and never think about what we have done. Develop an awareness of the things that you do.
- At the end of each hour, write down what you have done. It does not have to be in great detail – an outline suffices.
- Value what you have done, no matter how small or insignificant you feel it is.
- Identify some of the activities that can be made into a routine, such as the time you wake up, leave for work, have lunch, etc. This will help you recognise a pattern and build on it.
- Be creative and develop your own style of recording your activities.
- The activity schedule may be helpful in organising your day and change the way you do certain things. It can help you structure your day in a way that will help you to deal with your clutter.

Obstacles

'I am not working so I do not have a routine.'

You do not have to be working to make a structure. Write down what you do for a week, review the patterns and you will notice that you do have a routine.

'The things I do are not significant.'

We engage in activity for a reason and each has a function otherwise we would not do it.

'I find the activity schedule difficult to use.'

Develop your own recording system. Our template is just one of the ways you can record your activities. You may prefer to keep a journal. Use whatever is best suited for your needs.

Key messages

- Develop an awareness of the activities that you engage in, recognise them and write them down.
- Always remember that no activity is too small to be recorded.
- We engage in activity that provides a function. It is rare that we do things that have no personal purpose or significance.
- Everyone has a routine – recognise your routine and build on it.
- Develop your own personal recording system that is helpful for you.
- Knowing your baseline activity levels will help you develop an additional routine in your day to deal with your hoarding issues and clutter.

5

Hoarding flower I – behaviour

Each human being is unique and we all have our own way of dealing with our concerns. Yet we share common characteristics and having an understanding of the common elements of hoarding disorder provides us with the framework to work on our issues. We call this 'conceptualisation' in therapy. Conceptualisation – also known as formulation – is another term for gaining knowledge and then being able to make sense of your problems. Conceptualisation can also help you to explain why you behave in a certain way and illuminate the role this behaviour plays in maintaining your problem. When you conceptualise hoarding you will have a better idea of where to begin dealing with your problem, you will identify helpful and unhelpful behaviour and be able to make more informed choices of the kind of interventions to put into practice.

We will look at conceptualisation over the course of three chapters, beginning with behaviour here, moving to beliefs and finally tying both together with your emotions. We have done it this way to make it easier for you to understand how your behaviour, beliefs and emotions interconnect and play a role in maintaining your hoarding.

This is the first stage of making sense of your current problems. In the next chapter we will develop the conceptualisation further to identify past experiences that may have contributed to the development of your hoarding problem as well as possible vulnerabilities and the strengths that have helped you to cope so far. Conceptualisation forms your own understanding of the problem. It is dynamic and allows room for changes and testing out some of your assumptions in relation to your hoarding issues.

There are many ways of developing your formulation and, in our experience, developing a pictorial conceptualisation is most beneficial. We have discussed in previous chapters the value of using images in dealing with your hoarding problems. Additionally, writing or drawing enables you to relate to your formulation. That connection empowers you in making decisions about dealing with your hoarding issues.

The first step in developing your formulation is to name your problem. For the purpose of this book we have used the example 'my hoarding' but you can use whatever term you feel best fits for you and is something that you can relate to. It is not uncommon for individuals to have a name such as 'the bane of my life', 'my space-eater' or 'my clutter', etc. At the heart of the formulation lies your problem. It is also important to define what you lose as a result of that problem. We highlight the area of loss to help identify what you would like to recover. In the exercises that follow we use the example of the loss of space and a workable life. You can personalise your own losses as you work through the book.

Introducing the hoarding flower

In the illustrations on the next few pages you will see what we call the 'hoarding flower'. The centre of the flower represents your problem and the petals show the behaviour that maintains it. We behave in a way that deals with our feelings, emotions, fears and anxieties. From all behaviour flows a purpose with both short-term and long-term consequences. We often find that the immediate result is positive in that we feel better and may have a sense of relief. It's in the long-term impact that we see a negative consequence with the problem perpetuated and made worse.

Engaging and avoiding behaviour

There are two core behaviours in hoarding. The first is 'engaging behaviour' and includes collecting and saving items, internal recycling within the home and having a reason and justifying the need for things. The second, 'avoidant behaviour', includes not acknowledging that there is a problem, not dealing with clutter and not having justification or a reason for hoarding and doing other things instead. Both these types of behaviour play an active role in maintaining your hoarding issues.

Behaviour list

Let's start by making a list of all the behaviour associated with your hoarding. This may include collecting newspapers, not throwing things away and rationalising the need for items.

Hoarding flower I – behaviour

The behaviour associated with my hoarding is:

....

....

....

....

....

....

....

....

Next, take a fresh sheet of paper and write the term you use to describe your hoarding in the centre. We have decided to use the example of 'my hoarding' at the heart of our example formulation below. Under the title write the consequence of your hoarding and make it your personal experience. Draw a circle around the phrases:

My Hoarding

Loss of my space
and my life.

Now you will link your behaviour to your hoarding. Draw an arrow from the circle:

Choose one of the behaviours from the list you have composed above and write it above the arrow:

The short-term consequence of your behaviour is usually that you feel reassured and less anxious or distressed. The long-term impact is that your clutter increases and you maintain your hoarding problem. Now identify the consequences of each behaviour.

Hoarding flower I – behaviour

Having identified the consequences of one behaviour, draw another arrow feeding back to the centre to demonstrate how this maintains your hoarding. You can complete your own conceptualisation in the diagram below:

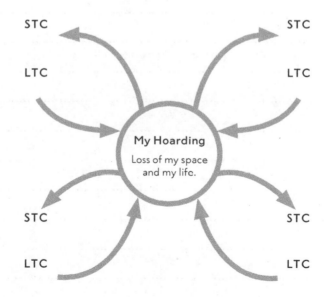

You have now made a conceptualisation of your hoarding with the hoarding flower.

My hoarding problem is maintained by my behaviour in:

....

....

....

....

....

....

....

....

....

....

....

....

....

....

....

....

....

Family and friends

You can aid understanding by asking questions to identify which behaviour is associated with hoarding. You can also discuss the short and long-term consequences and how the person concerned maintains the problem. Be aware that some people may consider this to be too personal and private and you can best help in such a situation by respecting the wishes of the person hoarding. Remember that we can sometimes be too involved in trying to assist. It may help to ask yourself what you think the other person really wants, as our desire to help, however well-meaning, can in itself become an obstacle to providing adaptive support. For some people, simply being around or making a hot drink may be the most effective support.

Tips

- Identify your behaviour as you move about your home, notice some of things that you do and write them down.
- Ask yourself, What does engaging in this behaviour do for me? What do I get out of it?
- Identify the things you avoid dealing with in terms of your clutter.
- Ask yourself, What is the reason that I am not dealing with this? What is holding me back? What is the reason for me being away from home?

- Identify the short-term and long-term consequences of your behaviour. Ask, What do I feel immediately? What happens in the long term? How is it helping me with my problem?'
- Use your formulation to guide you in how to deal with your hoarding behaviour. Focus on the long-term consequences. Remember – short-term gain means long-term pain.
- Review your formulation regularly, observe what has changed and rewrite your conceptualisation accordingly.
- Share your formulation with trusted family and friends. Going through it regularly will reinforce the way in which your behaviour impacts upon your space and life.

Obstacles

'I do not have the time to identify the behaviour I engage in.'

You do not need to make extra time for this. Observe what you do every day and write it down.

'How does making sense of my problems in relation to my behaviour help me?'

Having a good understanding of your problem and what keeps it going will help you make decisions about what you would like to change and where to start. This also helps you take responsibility for making changes to your space and your life.

'I do not want other people to see it.'

The formulation is personal and it is yours and you do not have to share it with others. You can decide whether you want to share it with family and friends. Sharing may help you to become more aware of the behaviour that keeps your problem going.

Key Messages

- Having an understanding of how your behaviour maintains your hoarding is beneficial.
- The hoarding flower is a road map to recovery, giving you the directions to reclaiming your space and your life.
- The hoarding flower will enable you to question the purpose and use of your behaviour.
- Keep the hoarding flower handy and revise it frequently. It is dynamic and it will change as you progress.
- Where possible, share the flower with others as it will help with deepening your understanding.

6

Hoarding flower II – beliefs

Our underlying beliefs can perpetuate and maintain our hoarding behaviours. We will discuss dealing with these beliefs in a later chapter. In this section, we will develop an understanding of how our beliefs contribute to the hoarding problem. We hold beliefs on everything – other people, the world and ourselves. Beliefs help us to function and relate to one another. But when beliefs are held rigidly, they start affecting us. For example, if we hold beliefs on recycling, these beliefs affect the way we discard items. When we are flexible, it is easier to discard the things that need to be got rid of. However, when the beliefs are held rigidly, it makes it more difficult as we place specific conditions on how things are to be recycled – often leading to items not being discarded. This is where techniques based on Cognitive Behavioural Therapy (CBT) can be useful, as discussed in part one of the book.

You may remember we said that CBT is based on the fact that our thoughts or beliefs affect the way we feel and react to a situation. For example, let's say you invite a friend over. When your friend arrives at your home they start clearing up and moving your things around. The next time your friend plans to visit, you may have thoughts that this friend is going to move things around again. These thoughts can cause you to feel anxious and lead you to either cancel the visit or to only allow your friend into an area that has the least clutter so that they don't interfere. CBT can help you to work on such beliefs so that you can deal with the anxiety. For the purposes of this book, we will also use the term 'beliefs' to encompass thoughts and assumptions.

Identifying beliefs

The first step is to name the beliefs that relate to our hoarding issues. You can do this as you start to deal with some of the things that you are hoarding by using a CBT technique called the 'downward arrow'.

An example of using the downward arrow: pick up an item that you are saving and attempt to get rid of it, asking yourself, what is preventing me in getting rid of this?

'I may need it.'

Imagine that you do need it and do not have it – what would that mean for you?

'I will be lost and will not be able to function fully.'

In order to be able to work with your beliefs it can be useful to change them into an 'if . . . then . . .' statement. This will enable you to address each point and develop a more adaptive belief. Convert the belief above, like this:

'If I do not have my things then I will not be able to function.'

Now you can test the validity of your beliefs based on

the conditions you have set. The example above assumes that the person's ability to function is based on having their things with them. In this case, testing out the belief would involve the person undertaking activities without having the things that they value with them and then checking the outcome. Were they able to function or was the prediction correct?

Identify your hoarding beliefs and express them as 'if . . . then. . . ' statements

Select an item from your hoard. Hold it and imagine that you need to throw it away. What is the immediate thought that comes to mind? An example might be 'I need it.' My thought about this object is:

....

....

....

....

....

....

....

....

....

....

Suppose this belief is true. What would it mean to me?

....

....

....

....

....

....

....

....

Suppose the above statement is true. What does it say about me? (For example, 'I can't cope'.)

....

....

....

....

....

....

....

....

Now convert the example above into an if . . . then . . . statement (for example, 'if I do not have my object then I will not be able to cope'):

If ....

....

....

....

....

....

....

....

Then ....

....

....

....

....

....

....

....

....

Repeat this for a number of behaviours that you identified in the previous chapter to help identify your beliefs. Focus on avoidant behaviour.

Make a list of all the beliefs that you have identified. The beliefs that I have identified as being associated with my hoarding are:

....

....

....

....

....

....

....

....

Take a fresh sheet of paper and, as you did in the last chapter, draw the centre of a hoarding flower in middle of the page, leaving space for the petals. Now write the title in the centre of the page and its consequences, as before:

My Hoarding

Loss of my space
and my life.

The next step is to link your beliefs to your hoarding problem. Draw an arrow out from the circle:

Now write a belief by the arrow:

If I do not have my things/items then I will not be able to function

My Hoarding

Loss of my space and my life.

As we saw in the previous chapter, the beliefs that you hold in relation to your hoarding produce two consequences, a short-term consequence (STC) and a long-term (LTC). At first you tend to feel better, reassured and less anxious. In the long term your hoard increases. The result of your behaviour associated with your beliefs is that you maintain your hoarding problem. Now write down the belief, associated behaviour and its consequences:

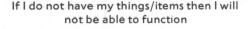

The diagram above demonstrates an example of one of the beliefs that drive your hoarding tendencies. You can develop your own conceptualisation below:

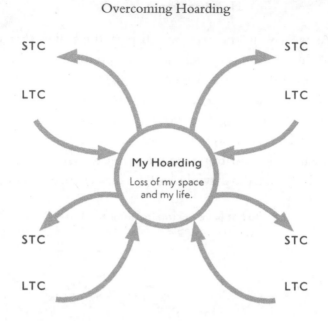

Now, having made a conceptualisation of your hoarding with the hoarding flower, how do you make sense of your associated beliefs and how do they maintain your problem?

My hoarding problem is maintained by my beliefs of:

....

....

....

....

....

....

....

....

....

....

....

....

....

....

....

....

....

Family and friends

As in the previous chapter, assessing or asking what level of support your family member or friend would like is key to deciding your input. Ways of helping might include contributing to identifying beliefs. Ask questions and use the downward arrow described in this chapter to find the meaning of thoughts and beliefs. Some people may need assistance in turning information into 'if . . . then . . . ' statements or with completing their hoarding flower. Remember for some just being present or being positive about the work they are doing can be invaluable.

Tips

- The best way to identify your beliefs is through working with the items that you are hoarding and the behaviours that you engage in.
- Be honest as you are dealing with your hoarding issues and it will be to your benefit.
- Do not feel that you have to get it 'right'. There is no right or wrong. You will know if you have identified the right belief, as it will feel right with you.
- Write down your beliefs when you identify them as it is easy to forget.

Obstacles

'I do not know where to start.'

Start by attempting to sort out the things that you are saving and by using the downward arrow.

'I do not know what to do.'

Ask a family member or friend to help you. They can ask you the downward arrow questions.

'I need a therapist to help me.'

The first step is to try it out yourself and you will find that you are able to identify your beliefs and notice that you do it all the time. Be your own therapist.

'I will get it wrong.'

Remember that there is no right or wrong. You are doing this for yourself and not for anyone else. It is likely that your belief that you need to get things right or be perfect is stopping you. If you feel that you might get it wrong, use the downward arrow to identify your belief and frame it in an 'if . . . then . . .' statement.

Key messages

- Understand the role of beliefs in the perpetuation of your hoarding problem.
- Identify these beliefs and address them to deal with your hoarding issues effectively.
- The behaviour associated with your hoarding is a good place to begin to identify the driving factors behind your problem.
- The downward arrow technique is a useful way to drill down from your initial thoughts about a situation to identify your underlying beliefs, assumptions and predictions. Once you have identified the beliefs, you can test them out.
- Using the downward arrow technique in all situations is a good way to develop your skills in identifying your beliefs.

7

Hoarding flower III – emotions and tying it all togther

In the previous two chapters, we started developing your hoarding flower formulation based on your behaviours and beliefs. Your emotions form another important component. Each person experiences a range of emotions subjectively. People find it difficult to tolerate negative emotions such as anxiety and distress – those sensations that, for the purposes of this book, we will call 'uncomfortable feelings'.

We engage in certain behaviours in an attempt to get rid of uncomfortable feelings. These behaviours, as discussed in the previous chapter, bring temporary relief but maintain the problem in the longer term. In a way, the behaviour we use to bring us relief can be described as 'short-term gain, long-term pain'. It is important to learn and develop healthier and better coping mechanisms that will enable us to live life fully. We will discuss ways of dealing with these negative emotions later.

It is easy to see why we use these behaviours to avoid feeling uncomfortable. As you work on your problems, try to be kind and patient with yourself in developing a compassionate view of your hoarding. Remember that there are other ways of coping with these uncomfortable feelings, but you will need to take risks and engage in other behaviour that may feel uncomfortable to begin with. It's not always easy to do that – we humans are by nature creatures of habit and tend to stick to what is known and feels safe.

Identifying feelings

Start by identifying the feelings that are related to your hoarding issues. The easiest way to identify your emotions is by picking up one of the things that you are saving and considering throwing it away.

How you are feeling as you pick up the item and consider throwing it away? I feel:

In which part of your body do you feel this feeling?

....

....

....

....

....

....

....

....

Ask yourself, What does this feeling mean to me?

....

....

....

....

....

....

....

....

Uncomfortable feelings are driven by our beliefs and maintained by the behaviour that we use to reduce their intensity. Write down the uncomfortable feelings that you experience when dealing with your hoarding issues.

....

....

....

....

Tying it all together

Now that you have identified the uncomfortable feelings, behaviours and beliefs, take a fresh sheet of paper and write your conceptualisation and its consequences in the centre, as we did in the previous chapter. Place a circle around the term as shown below:

My Hoarding
Loss of my space
and my life.

The next step is to link your feelings with your hoarding. Draw an arrow from the circle to link it with one of the behaviours, beliefs or uncomfortable emotions that you have identified.

Select one of those emotions and write it next to the arrow from the centre of your hoarding flower. An example of an emotion could be anxiety:

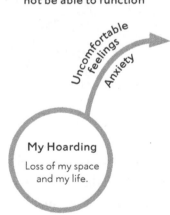

The uncomfortable feelings, beliefs and behaviours that are associated with your hoarding produce a short-term and a long-term consequence. In the short term you feel better, reassured, and less anxious or distressed. In the long term you have more clutter. The result is that by engaging in this behaviour, you maintain your problem. Now identify the consequences of each of your behaviours.

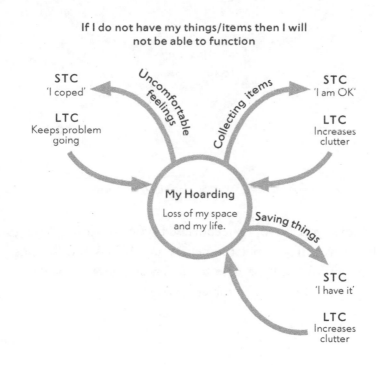

The diagram above demonstrates the uncomfortable feelings, beliefs and behaviours that drive your hoarding tendencies. Now develop and complete your own conceptualisation in the diagram below:

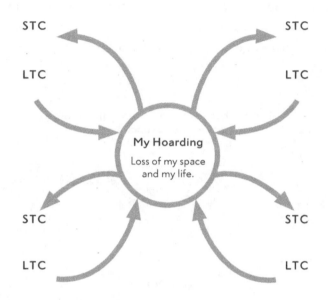

Now you have conceptualised your hoarding using the flower. If you put the behaviours, beliefs and feelings together you will be able to understand how they work together to keep your problem going.

My hoarding is maintained by these behaviours, beliefs and uncomfortable feelings:

....

....

....

....

....

....

....

....

....

....

....

....

....

....

....

....

....

....

....

Family and friends

We all experience uncomfortable feelings from time to time and we find ways to manage them. Some of these mechanisms are helpful and some are less so (such as avoiding them). Your role in relation to the person close to you can be to support and help them to sit with these uncomfortable feelings until they pass. Kindness and compassion can help your loved one to tolerate these difficult emotions and move forward with dealing with their problem. Think about – or ask them – what they need right now. It may be a hug, you being around or some kind words. Also consider what would not be useful, such as nagging or critical comments. Try to put yourselves in their shoes to understand how you can help and support them to sit with their uncomfortable feelings. Practical support such as asking questions to help to identify their beliefs and further developing their hoarding flower is likely to continue to be useful if this has helped in the earlier stages.

Tips

- Acknowledge the feelings that you experience in relation to your hoarding and identify the associated beliefs and behaviour that you engage in to cope with them.
- Do not avoid these feelings but learn to stay with

them, as the behaviour of trying to reduce them only perpetuates them.

- Write down your feelings – it is easy to forget them.

Obstacles

'I do not know where to start.'

Start by picking up an item that you are saving and notice and acknowledge how you are feeling. Locate where you feel it in your body and identify what it means to you.

'I do not know what to do.'

Ask a family member or friend to help you. Get them to support you when you have uncomfortable feelings. Ask yourself what these feelings mean to you.

'I need a therapist to help me.'

Start by trying it out yourself and you will find that you are able to identify your beliefs and you will notice that you do it all the time. Be your own therapist.

'I do not know what I am feeling.'

Remember that there is no right or wrong. You feel what you are feeling. You give your feelings a name and you decide what those feelings mean to you. Feelings may be uncomfortable, so be kind to yourself and accept them and they will pass. You can cope.

Key messages

- It is important to understand the role of behaviours, beliefs and feelings in the perpetuation of your hoarding problem.

- It is crucial to identify these behaviours, beliefs and feelings and address them so that you can deal with your hoarding issues effectively.
- Remember you are working towards reclaiming your space and your life.

8

Taking control of my problem – reclaiming flower

The last few chapters have focused on making sense of your problem. It is important to have a good understanding of your hoarding, especially the way in which it is perpetuated. This will help you to decide the best way to ensure progress.

Having made sense of your problem, it is time now to develop the way you reclaim your space with an exercise in which you will design a visual chart of the beliefs, emotions and behaviour you need to change. The reclaiming flower is a map of the factors that address your hoarding.

Let's start by making a list of those behaviours. You already have all the information you need – you'll find it in the hoarding flower exercises of the last three chapters. These are the areas that we will need to address.

Many of us find that after our environment has been cleared, whether we do it ourselves or others help, the clutter often builds up again. The aim of the reclaiming flower is to help you develop a way of reclaiming your space by dealing with each of the petals that maintain your problem. We often hear the term 'having to deal with the root of the problem' and it is certainly important for overcoming your difficulties. In this exercise we are attempting to deal with the factors that keep the hoarding problem going.

My beliefs, emotions and behaviours that maintain my problems are:

Beliefs	Emotions	Behaviours

Now you have a list of the elements that perpetuate your hoarding. The next step is to identify the replacement beliefs and behaviour that will provide a positive reinforcement for you in dealing with your clutter.

Make a note of the evidence that you have to support each belief. For example: belief – I can still function even if I don't have this item. Evidence – I have not seen or used this item for a long time and I am still able to function. I have not needed it to go about daily life.

Reclaiming flower

With your list of beliefs to hand, start with a fresh piece of paper. Write 'reclaiming my space and my life' in the middle and draw a circle around it. This is the heart of your reclaiming flower.

Reclaiming
my space
and my life

Next draw an arrow coming out from the centre of your reclaiming flower. Think up a new behaviour that will help you deal with your clutter. Examples include throwing things out on a daily basis or sorting items. Identify and write down the short-term and long-term consequences. For example, the short-term consequence of throwing things out could be a reduction in the amount of items and the long-term consequence would be the space being fully cleared of items.

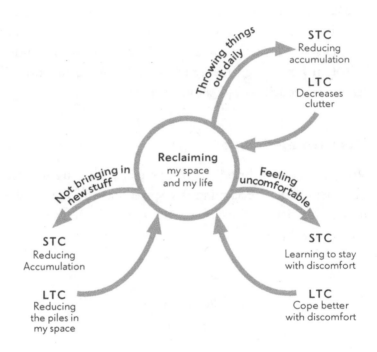

The exercise above gives you some examples of new behaviour that you could engage with to deal with your issues. The petals of the reclaiming flower can be formed by your new beliefs, emotions (how you would like to feel differently) and behaviour.

Identifying your new beliefs, emotions and behaviours

To identify your new set of beliefs in relation to your hoarding issues, first revisit your original vision of your new life. Make your vision as real as you can. If you find it difficult, use a photograph, a picture from a magazine or think about either a friend's home or somewhere you have visited before. As you visualise, ask yourself:

What does this feel like?

What does this feeling mean to me? What does it say about me?

In order to feel this way, what do I have to do differently?

If I behaved differently, what would the outcome be? What would that feel like? What would it mean to me or say to me?

My new beliefs, emotions and behaviours are:

New beliefs	New emotions	New behaviours

Insert the new beliefs, emotions and behaviours in your reclaiming flower.

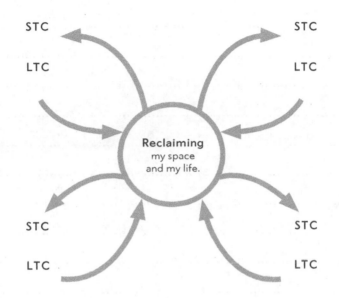

Now, having made a conceptualisation with the reclaiming flower, how do you make sense of the role played by these new elements in helping you reclaim your space and life?

My new beliefs, emotions and behaviours of

....

....

....

....

....

....

....

....

....

....

....

....

....

....

....

....

.... are the necessary changes that I have to make as part of my journey to reclaiming my space and my life.

Family and friends

You may have your own ideas about how you would reclaim space, but remember it is only the person with the hoarding problem who can take control and make the decisions about the steps they need to take. You can ask questions about their plans, encourage them to create an image of their vision or help them to draw the reclaiming flower and find a suitable place to display or keep it. If they find it difficult to create images, you can help by finding photos or by taking them to a friend's home to experience the benefits of greater space. You can also suggest ways they might express their new beliefs or describe their behaviour to make their intentions clear. Developing more adaptive and helpful beliefs to work towards and noting these down are key parts of reclaiming space and life. Creative ideas can be fun, motivating and uplifting for all and provide hope for the future.

Tips

- Revisit your vision to help you identify how you would like things to be different.
- Refer to your reclaiming flower on a daily basis to keep focused.
- If you meet an obstacle, refer to your reclaiming flower and the common examples below.
- As you progress, you will encounter further helpful

beliefs and behaviour. Address them and add them to the petals of your reclaiming flower.

- Display your reclaiming flower in an obvious place, such as on the front of your refrigerator, for easy access. It will be a constant point of reference.

Obstacles

'I cannot think of new beliefs, emotions or behaviour.'

Ask yourself what your vision is. If you achieved your vision, what would that feel like? In order to feel that way, what would you have to do differently? If you did things differently, what would that say or mean to you?

'I cannot visualise my original conceptualisation.'

Use photographs of an environment that you like, such as a friend's home or a place you have visited.

'I find it hard to feel different.'

Ask yourself, if you did not have a hoarding problem or your home was not cluttered, how would you feel? In what way would you feel different? What would this feeling mean to you?

Key messages

- Your vision is crucial to developing your reclaiming flower. It will help with motivation and moving in the right direction to deal with clutter.
- The reclaiming flower is an important part of your journey to reclaiming your space and your life.

- The reclaiming flower is the road map for your journey and will help you deal with the obstacles along the way.
- The reclaiming flower will reinforce your new, healthier beliefs, emotions and behaviour and help ensure consistency in your approach to dealing with your hoarding.
- The reclaiming flower gives you ownership of your recovery and helps maintain your focus.

9

Telling my story

We have looked at developing your formulation of your hoarding in terms of how your behaviour, beliefs and emotions maintain your problem. The formulation is focused in the moment, as things are now.

Now we can look at carrying out a review of your life to help manage difficulties associated with hoarding – and, indeed, many other problems. We may often seek the help of another person with a problem or a difficulty, whether a professional, a friend or a relative. We go to them with a story to tell. Often, we get asked about how we developed this problem, where it started and why it began. One very useful way of answering all those questions is through telling our own story.

Talking about hoarding is difficult. There are many reasons for this, not least that hoarding can be considered to be a taboo subject and is associated with feelings of embarrassment and shame. Yet there is a need to tell your story in order to help you make sense of it.

Your story is unique. It is yours and yours alone. It is fascinating. It comes with a range of emotions running from happiness to sadness. Telling it has a purpose and can be beneficial. However, we can also get into the habit of telling stories in a particular way that is unhelpful and which maintains our problems. This is particularly true when we talk about the past. If we tend to focus on the negative points of our story (a process known in therapy as rumination), this can have an impact on our mood, leaving us feeling depressed. To help us move on it is useful to keep balanced and focus on the elements which are positive and constructive.

There is a tendency for people to see their hoarding as being a part of them rather than as being a problem they can deal with. This can be reinforced further by the language used such as, 'I am a hoarder'. In this section we will look at how to tell your story in a way that helps you.

After completing each exercise it is useful to review it. Read over your work and take a moment to reflect on what you have done. This will help you develop a different perspective on what you believe and how you have viewed things. We often remember situations or events with clarity in the heat of the moment but the passage of time provides us with the ability to see things differently and can aid us in the process of moving on.

How to tell your story

There are a number of elements to consider when you think about how you talk about yourself:

What is your story about?

Who are the key players?

How does the plot unfold – what is the sequence of events?

What are the complications or complexities in the story and how they are resolved?

What happens in the end?

What have you learned?

When you are telling the story of your hoarding, it is important to separate yourself from your problem. It is as if you take what you are describing from inside yourself and put it next to you. You need to step away to gain a sense of perspective. The result is you will see yourself as a person who has a problem rather than as a problem person.

You will notice that when your hoarding problem is not inside, you can deal with it much more readily. You should feel less overwhelmed and more able to develop a plan of action for dealing with your hoarding. All you need to do is change the words you use when you describe your condition in order to loosen your personal attachment. Let's look at an example:

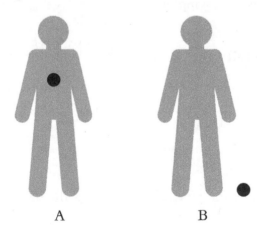

A   B

In our example, person A sees the problem as an integral part of their being. Their language will reflect this: 'I'm a hoarder. Things get really bad sometimes and I get really depressed.'

Now let's hear person B. Can you tell that they are a separate entity from their problem . . . just by their use of language? 'The hoarding causes me a lot of problems and if the depression makes an appearance, things can get even worse.'

We use language and metaphor as a tool to help us make sense of and manage our difficulties. For example, if you find yourself saying, 'My hoarding is like a millstone around my neck,' that gives you an idea of the difficulties you are experiencing as a result of your problem. You can gain greater understanding and a better perspective by looking back at your whole life rather than simply focusing on the present difficult situation. When we feel overwhelmed we have a natural tendency to blot out the achievements and positive events in our lives. It can be helpful to remind ourselves.

Think about a recent situation which made you angry or annoyed or frustrated. Write a brief story about what happened, who was involved and what unfolded.

....

....

....

....

....

....

....

....

....

....

....

....

....

....

Now check you have used all the key elements in telling your story:

What is the story about?

Who are the key players?

How does the plot unfold – what is the sequence of events?

What are the complications or complexities and how are they resolved?

What happens in the end?

What have I learned from this story?

Life review

A life review can be a useful tool in telling your story comprehensively. In such an exercise, you will find that you compare the past and the present – which is normal. You will reflect and reminisce and this will evoke certain feelings. Note down the feelings as they will help you to make sense of situations you have encountered in your life.

Occasionally, writing your life review may bring up emotions that you find difficult to manage. You may feel overwhelmed. One way to help you to manage your emotions is to limit the time that you spend writing to, say, thirty minutes and then plan something to do that helps you to cope with the thoughts and feelings evoked. You could write every day at a set time in your routine and follow that with a planned reward activity, such as going for a walk with a friend or listening to music. In the event that very difficult issues or feelings arise you may need to seek professional help from your doctor or a suitably qualified practitioner. Please see the appendix for further details of help that is available. When you feel ready to continue with the exercise, read the instructions below.

Find somewhere comfortable and safe to sit quietly where you will not be disturbed or distracted. Remember to have your pad and pencil ready. Relax, take a deep breath, close your eyes and breathe out. Clear your mind of worries. Read the questions below one at a time and then make some notes. Afterwards, share your stories with a family member or friend and make a note of how you felt about the whole exercise.

Age	Question for review
Childhood	What is the first thing you remember as a child? Where were you? And who do you remember being present?
	Did you have brothers and sisters or other family members? What was each one like when you were a child?
	Do you remember outings, day trips or holidays as a child? What kind of things did you do in your leisure time? Where did you go? Who did you go with?
	Do you remember being sick or having any accidents?
Adolescence	What was it like growing up in your town as a teenager?
	Which people were important to you? Family? Teachers? Friends? Write about each one.
	Did you work as a teenager?
	What was the worst thing about being a teenager in your town?
	Can you remember having to deal with something really tough or difficult as a teenager?
Family and home	What was your home town like? What were your favourite places there?
	What were the happiest times you can remember at home?

	Which member of your family are you most like?
Adulthood	Think of two important events in your adult life. Write about them. Who was involved? Where did they take place?
	Did you form significant friendships during this time?
	Did you work at this time? What did you do?
	Do you think people and relationships in your life have changed over the years?
	What's the best thing about being the age you are now?

Once you have completed the exercise, read it through and reflect on how this made you feel and what you learned from it.

How did reviewing my life make me feel?

....

....

....

....

....

....

....

....

What did I learn from it?

....

....

....

....

....

....

....

....

....

....

Reflecting on your whole life gives you a sense of context. Placing your current problem in your timeline gives you a better understanding of it. This puts you in a better position to separate you from your difficulties and helps you to recognise your strengths and skills in dealing with hoarding.

'Dear Hoarding'

Writing a letter to your hoarding problem may feel strange but it is a useful exercise that could help you overcome some of your obstacles. As before, find a quiet safe place, where you will not be distracted or disturbed. Take a few breaths to clear your mind of concerns. Start your letter by addressing your hoarding problem directly with 'Dear Hoarding'. Take your time – write about what the problem means to you, how it has affected your life and include the positives as well as the negatives.

After completing the letter, read it, review it and reflect on it. There are elements you might want to revisit to see if you can view them differently. Here are some key questions to help you to unpack your letter.

What do I understand about my hoarding?

....

....

....

....

....

....

....

....

....

....

....

Where and when did my hoarding start?

....

....

....

....

....

....

....

....

How has my hoarding kept going all this time?

....

....

....

....

....

....

....

....

What can I do about it?

....

....

....

....

....

....

....

....

Writing this letter will help you make the links between how and when your problems began, the impact they have had on your life and what you wish to do about them.

Family and friends

The process of telling a life story or writing a letter addressed directly to the hoarding can be difficult and emotional as well as a very powerful way to connect and make sense of life experiences. You may be welcomed as a witness or the individual may wish to read their letter to you. Others may regard this as very personal and private and it's vital to respect their wishes. If their attention is fixed on difficult times and memories, you can help by highlighting positive experiences. Suggesting a pleasurable or rewarding activity after a planned period of writing may help to support the person close to you in this process.

Tips

- Spend some time thinking about and writing your story.
- Write down the main points and use the guide in this chapter to help you construct the story.
- Recognise that the language you are using, the way in which you talk about yourself, has an effect.
- There is no right or wrong; it is your story.
- Share your story with those you trust.
- Everyone has a story to tell. The narrative helps us make sense of our experiences.
- Telling stories is a normal part of life.
- The use of stories helps us relate to ourselves, others and the world.
- Stories are a medium that makes us feel connected with others.
- Remember the positive experiences as they are often disregarded.

Obstacles

'I do not have a quiet place to write.'

If you don't have somewhere suitable at home, your quiet place can be the library, a café, the park or a friend's house. It need only be a space in which you feel comfortable and where you know there will be reduced disturbance or disruptions.

'I cannot remember the past.'

Be patient and gentle with yourself. As you start writing – your story, life review or a letter – you will find that you will recall memories of the past. Do not have the expectation that you will remember everything. You will find that your memories will float in when you least expect it.

'What if it is too upsetting for me?'

It may be upsetting, but that is not a negative experience. The emotion will help you remember how you have dealt with things in the past and will make you aware of your resilience in dealing with difficult situations. It may be helpful, after undertaking this task, to engage in a relaxing activity or meet up with friends or family.

Key messages

- Telling your story can be a powerful tool, particularly in trying to understand how your problems develop.
- When you write your story yourself, you have control over the pace and how you would like it to be told.

- The words you choose will affect the impact your story makes on you.
- Telling your story is a cathartic process, as it allows you to express and release your feelings and, in the process, work through them.
- Telling your story will help you learn to focus on the positive aspects of your experiences that can be overlooked in the face of your difficulties.

10

The grid method

We hope that you have found the exercises in the previous chapters have given you the opportunity to make sense of your problem.

Working with the hoarding flower will have helped you to make connections between your beliefs, your feelings and your behaviour. Telling your story links the past, present and future in relation to your hoarding. Your vision points to where you would like to go. This is an important process, as CBT relies on having an understanding of what triggers and perpetuates problems. This insight allows you to work on your problems and decide on the most appropriate interventions. Many of your questions about your current issues can be answered as a result.

Now that we have concluded the formulation of both the problem and the recovery, from this chapter onwards we will be looking at interventions that you can use with hoarding.

When we look at our environment and see it is cluttered, we often end up feeling overwhelmed. This can lead to us giving up before we have started to work on our problems. We feel immobilised and engage in avoidant behaviour such as staying away from the space altogether.

We might busy ourselves with other activities, leaving the clutter unmanaged.

One way of managing this feeling is to work on a particular area that will bring comfort to you at this moment. Ask yourself, Which space would make the biggest difference to me? For example, you may not have a place to sleep, so the bedroom may be most significant as any improvement will allow you to rest. Yet even one area may appear dauntingly large at first if you are feeling overwhelmed. You can cope with this by dividing the area into smaller sections using a grid. In the instructions that follow we will show you how to make smaller sections that enable you to work on your clutter in a more effective way.

Identify the overall space

The significant area that I have chosen is

....

....

....

....

....

....

....

....

Draw a diagram of your significant area/room. A square or rectangle is usually sufficient. Draw roughly where your furniture is currently placed in the room. Then divide the room into smaller areas by drawing lines both horizontally and vertically:

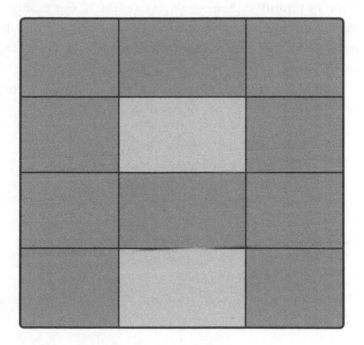

Each square or rectangle represents an area that you are going to work on. Compared to looking at the whole space, a single bite-sized chunk of grid will be less threatening. The area that you need to de-clutter will be as a result smaller and more manageable.

Grid categories

Let's list the items that are within your first small area and their importance to you. For example, there may be books, magazines, papers and clothes. List these items in terms of categories rather than as individual items. Order the list in terms of priority to help you work on them. For example, among the items mentioned above, your priority may be to de-clutter the papers, followed by magazines, books and lastly clothes.

Now that you have your smaller area identified in your grid, the broad categories of items are:

a.

b.

c.

d.

e.

Now rate your categories from one to five, with one being the easiest and five the most difficult to discard.

1.

2.

3.

4.

5.

The grid method

You can now be systematic in dealing with the most manageable items first rather than getting stuck dealing with things that you find difficult (which in turn reduces your capacity to clear the area). You will find that you develop a pattern of sorting and reducing your clutter that will help when you later deal with the more difficult items.

As discussed in other sections, enlisting the help of family and friends may be very helpful when you begin de-cluttering, particularly when dealing with areas that are more difficult.

Use your activity schedule as a way to work consistently on a daily basis.

Family and friends

Those you support may value talking through which area is the most significant to start on and the benefits in clearing it. Support them by preparing their grid system, developing the hierarchy to make tasks less overwhelming and making sure they don't get too weighed down in the detail of determining categories. If the person wishes to contact you with their aims for the day, try to enable this by whatever method suits you both. It may be that being present when the more difficult decisions are being made will assist in the disposal of items. Again, provide encouragement in noting progress and making changes to the grid. Noticing improvements, however small, is likely to be rewarding. Ask how your friend or family member is using their reclaimed space.

Tips

- Walk around your significant space and get a feel for it – develop a map in your mind.
- If there is no obvious working space, start from wherever you can, say the entrance, and work your way methodically into the room.
- Do not spend too much time worrying about the items that are saved in each section – a broad category will suffice.
- Locate the nearest recycling bins, find the time of rubbish collection and use the bins to your advantage when getting rid of the things that have cluttered your space.
- Get friends or family to support you with the difficult items in your hierarchy.
- Identify what you find to be the most helpful approaches when working with your clutter.
- Write down what you have done and review your grid, redrawing it to show the spaces that have been cleared.
- Ensure that you work on an identified area. Do not move from one area to another. By working consistently in one grid you will see the clutter reducing and also this will create hope that things are changing.
- Ensure that the de-cluttered items move out of your environment. Commonly, people deal with their clutter by moving it from room to room. This is often called 'internal recycling' or 'churning'. It is not

helpful as it maintains your hoarding – we will deal with that in chapter nineteen, Traps.

- Each time you leave the house, take a bag out to discard or give away. This will help you develop new patterns of dealing with your clutter.

- Contact a friend or family member you trust, inform them of your intention for the day and call them later to let them know of your progress. If you are not able to contact anyone, write down your intention and at the end of the day review and update with progress.

Obstacles

'I do not know where to start.'

Walk around the space and draw your grid. Being in the space will help you decide where you can begin. It may be helpful to start at the entrance and work your way into the room to create space.

'There are too many things in the space to develop a hierarchy.'

Do not be concerned about the details – just use broad categories such as magazines, books and newspapers. Don't get bogged down in listing specific types or titles.

'Some of the items are too difficult to deal with.'

Leave the harder items for another time and move them to another area – deal with what is easiest first. Come back to the difficult items later, when you have developed further skills and have some support.

'I have difficulty making decisions.'

It is normal to feel that you are not able to make decisions and fear that you might make the wrong choice. Come back to the difficult decisions later and do not let them become an obstacle. As you work through this book you will learn ways of making decisions and working with your beliefs.

Key messages

- Use a grid to break down the significant area that you are planning to work on into smaller and more manageable sections.
- Develop your hierarchy – it will help you to deal with the easiest items first and help you to develop your skills in de-cluttering.
- Write down your own tips and key phrases that you have found helpful when de-cluttering.
- Celebrate the space you have reclaimed by spending time in it and embracing the feeling.
- Use your vision and the work done with the H.O.A.R.D. tool (see p. 60) to motivate you.

11

Clutter image rating scale

Being overwhelmed can stop some people in their tracks and this is often one of the reasons why people avoid dealing with their hoarding. All too often, the environment is so cluttered that people end up unable to start work. The grid method has been found to be useful to identify a small area to work on which is more manageable and maintains the focus of the work that needs to be undertaken.

Our colleagues in the USA have developed a visual measure or rating tool, the clutter image rating scale[2]. Clinicians use the scale to assess the severity of clutter in a person's home. This visual scale ranges from one to nine in degrees of clutter. The scale has been developed for use in the different rooms of a home and is easily accessible on the internet. A copy is available for you to use in the appendix (see p. 344).

---

2 Frost, R. O., Steekee, G., Tolin, D. and Renaud, S. (2008). 'Development and validation of the clutter image rating'. *Journal of Psychopathology and Behavioural Assessment*, 30 (3): 193–203

Clutter Image Rating: Bedroom

Please select the photo that most accurately reflects the amount of clutter in your room.

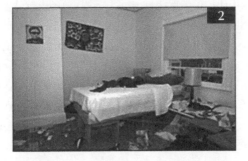

Clutter image rating scale

(7—9 continued on next page)

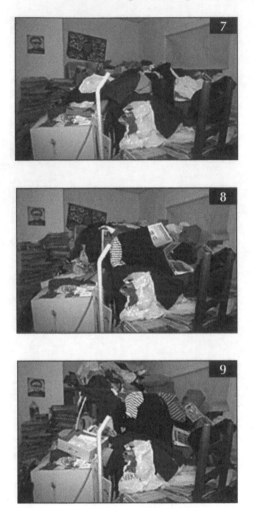

The image provides an individual with a sense of what the room would look like once cleared. It is very much like the vision you created in the exercises early in part two. How it differs, though, is that where your vision was based on self-generated imagery, this tool uses photographs which are less abstract and more concrete – making it easier to relate to. The area is regularly measured to provide a record of changes.

The added benefit of using the scale is that you yourself (rather than a clinician) undertake the assessment by rating the severity of clutter within your environment. You remain in control and the images of cluttered rooms are useful in this respect as they allow you to compare your own environment with that in the photographs. This scale is easy to use and does not need any specialist training. All you need to do is choose the image that best represents the appearance of your living space. You can use the tool to plan the steps for reducing clutter. This is a step-by-step approach.

Using the scale

Once you have downloaded a copy of the clutter image rating scale, take it into the environment that you are planning to clear. Use the scale to rate the area that you identified in the grid in the previous chapter. When you have made an assessment, ask yourself how you would like the room to look, given the time and opportunity that you have for de-cluttering. Be realistic about how much you are able to achieve. Make a record of how you would like the room to look at the end of that period by referring to the scale and choosing the most appropriate photo – note the rating. Next, ask yourself what steps you would need to take in order for the area to reach that end point. Write the steps as a plan and incorporate them within your activity schedule.

Rate your room

Once you have identified your space using the grid method, as outlined in the previous chapter, use the scale to rate an area in terms of the severity of the clutter.

Using the clutter image rating scale, the space that I have identified to work on has a rating of:

....

....

....

....

....

....

....

....

Refer again to the scale to work out how you would like the space to look over the next week. Remember to be realistic about what you are able to achieve during that period of time.

Clutter image rating scale

In the next week I would like the space to look like the photo on the scale that has a rating of:

....

....

....

....

....

....

....

Now that you have both the initial image and a lower rating, you need to develop a plan of action.

My plan of action is:

....

....

....

....

....

....

....

....

Incorporate this plan into your activity scheduling sheet to ensure that you make the time to work on this area. Take a photograph of the area before you start working on it or draw the layout of the space and shade the area with your pen if you can't take a photo.

It is also important to have your own criteria by which you can judge that you have achieved what you had planned.

I will know that I have achieved the revised rating of:

....

....

....

....

....

....

....

....

because the space will have:

....

....

....

....

Clutter image rating scale

....

....

....

....

....

Keep a record of what you have removed from the space. Take a photograph to help you review this at a later time. If you are not able to take a photograph, redraw the area and shade in the location of your items. As with the photographs, you can use drawings to review changes.

Family and friends

The images of the clutter image rating scale can help you objectively assess the progress being made by the person close to you. If asked, you may be able to provide practical help by printing off the scale or enabling access to the internet. Provide help to plan and to identify obstacles to progress by reviewing the images and rating the current situation. It may be useful to help display the scale in a prominent place in the home if that is the wish of the person who is dealing with hoarding. Encourage them to use the scale as part of the whole package of tools to facilitate making changes.

Tips

- Be realistic about how much you can achieve in the given timeframe.
- Keep the clutter image rating scale in a place where it can remind you of the target you would like achieve.
- Carry out regular reviews using the scale and remind yourself of your timeframe to help you motivate yourself.
- Review your criteria if your target is difficult to achieve.
- Ask your friends or family to support you with this task.
- Have a consistent approach to working on the identified area.
- Design your plan to deal with your clutter as part of your daily activity schedule – this will ensure that you are working on it on a regular basis.
- Mark 'before' and 'after' points on the scale with an arrow to highlight how you would like your environment to look in the end.
- How will you know what you have achieved? Have a benchmark in mind and write it down.
- Keep a record of what has been removed from the area.

Obstacles

'I cannot access the clutter image rating scale.'

The scale is easily accessible on the internet. If you do not have a computer, go to the local library to access a computer to print out a copy. There is also a copy of the scale at the back of this book. Family or friends may help you.

'I do not know what steps I need to take.'

Initially, it may be difficult to consider the steps that you need to take to deal with your clutter. It may be useful to read the next few chapters first before returning to this section and using the clutter scale to help you design your plan of action. Do not let this initial difficulty prevent you from working on your hoarding issues.

'How will I know that I have achieved a lower rating for the space?'

First of all, you have the photographs on the scale that will provide you with a guide for how you would like the space to look. You have also set out your own personal criteria. This will help you identify the point you consider similar to the lower-rated image in the scale.

Key messages

- Use the clutter image rating scale as an additional tool to work out a planned approach to dealing with your clutter.
- The scale will enable you to rate the degree of your clutter consistently.
- Be realistic about what you can achieve in a timeframe. Being over-ambitious and not meeting your target will lead you to feel disappointed and despondent.

- Be consistent in your approach. Refer back to the scale as the visual images are powerful reminders of how you would like your environment to look.
- Use your vision and the H.O.A.R.D tool (see p. 60) to help with your motivation.

12

Yes/no/maybe

A common complaint among those who have hoarding issues is that they find it difficult to make decisions about de-cluttering. It is understandable that no one wants to make a bad move by losing material they may need in the future. But often we hang on to things and rarely refer to them again. Life is about taking risks. Taking risks can help us cope better as it teaches us new and more adaptive ways of dealing with situations.

Decisions can be made based on our emotions. Emotions are not facts about the world and they can distort our perception. Each and every one of us is aware of the things we need or do not need, but when a decision has to be made we develop doubts which can result in paralysis. These doubts are fuelled by our beliefs and emotions. A similar situation also occurs when we have too many choices about what to do with things and find it hard to act.

One way to help is to sort out items into three different piles. The first contains items that can definitely be discarded – 'yes'. The 'no' pile is for items that cannot be discarded and the 'maybe' stack is for those things you're not sure about. The three choices make it easier when having to discard items that have been hoarded. The easiest decisions are made for the 'yes' and 'no' piles, while you can return to the 'maybe's later to make the decision.

You will find that using these three categories will make it easier for you to work on your clutter and reduce the risk of inaction by procrastination. It is always useful to have clear criteria for each type of item. For example, an individual sorting out paper clutter may decide that newspapers can be discarded (the 'yes' pile) if they have not been read for a certain period – say, in the last month – or if they are bills that have been paid over a year ago. The 'no' papers might be work-related, or paperwork needed for tax details and so on. Further thought could be given to the 'maybe' pile.

Three piles

As you work on your selected area using the grid approach discussed in chapter ten, create three separate piles for 'yes', 'no' and 'maybe'. Ensure that you have a black bin-bag or any other bag that you wish to use. Keep the bag there so you can dispose of items immediately and reduce the risk of creating an attachment to anything that you have selected to discard.

One way to help decide quickly is to allocate yourself three seconds; this is often referred to as the three-second rule. Take just three seconds to rule on whether an item stays or goes. When dealing with papers, it might also be useful to have a few folders handy. You can place the papers directly in the relevant folders if you are intending to keep them.

Look at the items on the hierarchy, discussed in chapter ten, that are within the area that you have chosen to work in. Select the easiest to discard category and establish the 'yes' and 'no' criteria for those items. It is always helpful to have the details prominently displayed in your working area so that you can refer to them.

My criteria for the items that can be discarded ('yes' pile):

....

....

....

....

....

....

....

My criteria for the items that cannot be discarded ('no' pile):

....

....

....

....

....

....

....

Acting on your criteria

Now that you have identified the rules for 'yes' and 'no', write them down and place them by their respective piles. Ensure that you have a bag ready for 'yes' items that are to be discarded. Maintain distance between the piles so that you can differentiate between them easily. It may be helpful to place different coloured cards on each.

Begin to pick up items that are on the lowest rating on your hierarchy. Quickly scan the item and ensure you are familiar with your rules. Do not spend an excessive amount of time deciding. The longer you spend, the more difficult you will find it to discard the item. This is because looking at the item makes it more likely that you will attach emotional significance and value to it. You will recognise how we often talk ourselves into doing or not doing something.

If items are placed in the 'maybe' pile, leave them there. Once you have cleared the space completely, revisit both the 'no' and 'maybe' piles and again divide them into the three categories. This time, allow a slightly longer time to consider whether each item is worth saving. This process of refining will help you in two ways: firstly, by ensuring that only the items you really need are saved and secondly by helping you develop new and more efficient skills in decision making.

Family and friends

Consistently using the terms 'yes', 'no' and 'maybe' will help to reinforce the work in creating the three piles. Speed in decision-making is important, so helping with clear criteria and offering support when the sorting and clearing is in progress can really help the person close to you. Explain the decision you would make in the same situation – if they seek your advice. Decisions ultimately need to be made by the family member or friend but practical help can be of great benefit – you can provide black bags or help to make space. You may find that your support is most welcome when your friend or family member returns to the 'maybe' and 'no' piles for the second time, when the choice becomes tougher.

Tips

- Make the criteria for the 'yes' and 'no' piles of items brief and simple.
- Be quick in reviewing your items. The longer you spend looking and checking, the more likely you are to retain the items, as you will form stronger attachments.
- Be practical and do not rely on emotion to make decisions.
- Step into a friend or family member's shoes and

consider what they would do when having to make the same decision.

- Identify the broad category of items in each area you clear.
- Once an item has been designated a 'yes', place it directly into the appropriate bin-bag. Try to avoid rechecking as this will create doubts and you may try to keep the item.
- If the item is placed in the 'no' pile, place it there and leave it as it is for the moment.
- Revisit 'maybe's and 'no's.

Obstacles

'I cannot decide on the criteria.'

Observe what others might use as criteria to guide them in saving or discarding things. Imagine if your closest friend or family member was having to make the same decision and asked for your advice. What you would say to them?

'Some of the items are too difficult to deal with.'

Some things may be too difficult, so leave them for another time. Do not spend time pondering as it will only strengthen your conviction that an item has to be kept. Come back to the difficult items later when you have the skills and some support.

'I have difficulty making decisions.'

It is normal to feel that you are not able to make decisions and fear that you might make the wrong decision. If you are finding it hard to make a decision, it is most likely based on your feelings or emotions. Ask yourself, If I presented this decision to a friend, what would they say? Or, If a friend presented this to me what would I say to him or her?

Key messages

- You tend to keep to decisions that are made based on your emotions or feelings.
- Dividing items into 'yes', 'no' and 'maybe' piles can be a useful way to de-clutter your space.
- Revisit 'no' and 'maybe' to further reduce the items that you are saving or hoarding.
- Keep the checking as brief as possible. The longer you check, the more likely the item will not be discarded.
- The more you practise, the easier it will become.
- Keep in mind your vision and use the image of how you would like your space and your life to be.

13

Self-talking

Over time you have probably attempted to deal with your hoarding problems. You have most likely experienced negative, distressing emotions when faced with the necessity to discard items. In coping with these emotions, you may have found that you convinced or tricked yourself into keeping certain items. In this book we refer to this as your 'self-talk'. You self-talk when you convince yourself not to do what needs to be done as a means of reducing your level of discomfort. The good news is that you can use this self-talk in a positive way to help deal with your hoarding problem.

This approach uses Cognitive Behavioural Therapy (CBT). This involves looking at your thinking and starting to question the way you perceive situations. You will gain some of the skills needed to deal with your beliefs, as discussed with regard to your hoarding flower (see chapters 5–7). CBT helps to explain the role of thinking in the way we feel (emotions) and in how we deal with a situation (behaviour). For example, if we believe that by saving things we will be safe and secure, the moment there is any threat to that belief – things being taken away – we experience negative emotions and react with particular behaviour.

So we try to cope with the negative emotions or engage in behaviour to prevent what we believe will happen as a consequence.

To illustrate this, imagine you have a belief that gaining knowledge is very important and that knowledge is gained through keeping up to date and reading. It is very likely that you will keep all material that pertains to knowledge – newspapers, magazines and books – as you feel that you will need to read them all.

Thinking back to your hoarding flower exercises, you can see how your beliefs, emotions and behaviours interact and affect each other. In order to deal with your hoarding problem it is important to target each of those components. De-cluttering alone will not deal with the underlying mechanisms that maintain your hoarding. Those of us who have experienced our homes or environment being cleared by external agencies (for example, environmental health or housing departments) will have felt extreme distress and noticed that over a period of time the environment becomes cluttered again. People hoard or save things for a reason. You can think about it as a coping mechanism. In Telling my Story (chapter nine) you may have uncovered the reason that you hoard.

Our self-talking CBT technique involves challenging thoughts and beliefs. Instead of convincing yourself to save something, you are developing the skill of talking yourself into not saving the item. The self-talk questioning is aimed at looking at the facts and helping you to achieve a more balanced view of things. The skill of self-talk questioning can be transferred to other situations that you encounter on a daily basis.

Questioning through self-talk

When you attempt to discard an item, you may find that it is difficult. You will notice the self-talk kicks in as you convince yourself to keep it. Having the ability to recognise this as self-talk is important because, at this point, you will need to intervene and adapt the self-talk to better deal with your clutter and hoarding issues. When you recognise that you are beginning to convince yourself that you need to keep an item, use that recognition to ask yourself some questions:

- When was the last time I looked at this item?
- If I had not found it, would I have remembered it?
- How likely is it that I am going to use it?
- When was the last time I used it? Do I remember using it?
- By not having it, is my life deficient in any way?
- If this item was lost or stolen, would I not be able to function?

Below are some of the key questions that you can use when you are dealing with de-cluttering your environment. As you ask yourself these questions, you will find that the automatic self-talk will kick in to convince you that you need the item. For example:

Q: When was the last time I looked at this item?

A: A long time ago.

Q: If it was a long time ago, do I really need it?

A: I may need it in the future; I have paid money for it and it would be a waste to give it away and later on have to buy it again.

Q: What would be the best thing for me to do?

A: I need to keep it.

This is the point you will need to intervene as you become aware and notice the self-talk kicking in.

Q: When was the last time I looked at this item?

A: A long time ago.

Q: If it has been a long time, do I really need it? How likely is it that I am going to use it?

A: It is possible I might need it, but I have not looked at it for a long time; it is unlikely that I will need to use it.

Q: How useful is it for me to keep it and what does it do for me?

A: Keeping it only adds to my clutter and it does not help me with my hoarding issues.

Q: If I did not have it, would it make a difference to my life?

A: I have had it all this time and it has not made a difference. It has only added to my clutter and if I had not just found it, I would not have remembered it.

Q: If I need it in the future, what can I do?

A: I could borrow it from a friend and, in the worst-case scenario, I might have to buy it. Given that I have not used it in all this time, it is unlikely that I will need to use it in the immediate future.

Self-talk is a very powerful tool that people can use to either perpetuate or help overcome their problems. The above example demonstrates how the same situation can be dealt with using different forms of self-talk.

Question and response

It is important to start using the self-talk questioning each time you are dealing with your clutter. A good way to practise this is to write down each question and response. The rationale for this is that it will help you distance yourself emotionally from the things you are dealing with and enable you to start considering the situation from a different perspective.

Pick up an item that you are sorting out and ask yourself: What is the significance of this item to me?

Follow this question with some of the other questions as

discussed above. Be creative and develop your own questions that are specific to your situation.

If you find yourself in a situation that is difficult, enlist the support of a friend or family member who can help with the questioning. When you ask for this support, be mindful that the friend or family member is there to help you and they are not attempting to cause you distress or upset you with their questioning.

Family and friends

If you are with your friend or family member when they are sorting, it may be helpful to ask what is going through their minds if you see them hesitating about which of the 'yes', 'no' and 'maybe' piles an item should go in. This is likely to be the moment when they self-talk. Hopefully, they can develop more adaptive self-talk in time but for now encourage them to write down the questions to distance them from the difficult emotions they experience in letting an object go. Being available should they meet an obstacle (if they find it hard to develop more useful self-talk) can help. You can ask questions about when they last used or needed an item and what they could do in the future, as described in the exercises above. While remembering that the decision is theirs, suggesting alternatives to choose from can sometimes help when working with beliefs and self-talk. We all have different perspectives and tend not to think of other options unless we deliberately focus on doing so and step back from our emotions.

Tips

- Be aware of when you self-talk and how it perpetuates your hoarding.
- Write down each time you engage with self-talk. If you are finding reasons to keep your items, then question yourself, step by step. It is good practice to develop your skills in self-questioning.
- If you are having difficulties, ask a friend or family member to ask you the questions.
- Step back from your problem to gain some emotional distance from the situation. This will help you to think differently about the things you save.
- Use self-talk questioning when you notice that you are finding reasons to keep items.
- Write down the self-talk questions and answers.
- While working on the practical aspects of de-cluttering, addressing the underlying mechanisms is an effective way to deal with your hoarding problem.

Obstacles

'I do not know when to question myself.'

The moment that you notice you are starting to find reasons to keep an item is a good time. Write down your reasons and question yourself in a step-by-step way.

'I do not know what to ask myself.'

There is no right or wrong way to question yourself. Bring to mind your vision and your intention to de-clutter and use that as a guide to help you. The aim is to consider the significance and consequences of your hoarding behaviour. Imagine that you are helping someone else and that you are asking them the questions. Write the questions as it helps to focus on what you are asking.

'What if I still want to keep my items?'

If, after using the self-talk questioning, you still want to keep the item, put it to one side and return to it later. It may be helpful to ask a friend or family member to help with your self-talk questioning so that you can step back from your attachment to the item.

Key messages

- Self-talk can be used positively to help you with the underlying mechanisms that keep your hoarding problem going.
- Self-talk questioning will address the beliefs that are related to hoarding.
- Writing questions will help you develop your skills in stepping back and challenging your thoughts and beliefs.
- Revisit your vision and the H.O.A.R.D. tool associated with the photographs of your environment as a way to motivate yourself.

14

Questioning and beliefs

In the last chapter we discussed using self-talk positively while working with the 'yes', 'no' and 'maybe' groupings as a way to de-clutter. Using self-talk is a good way to start working with your beliefs. CBT proposes that our beliefs are formed as a result of our experiences. For example, let's say you once went to a restaurant where the food was not of good value and quality. When a friend later suggests going there for a meal, you would immediately think, 'That restaurant does not provide good value for the money they charge'. This is a good example of how an inference or interpretation has been made based on your belief about the restaurant which was formed based on your past experience. The way we feel or react behaviourally is based on the interpretation we make of the situation we are in.

If you recall, chapters 5–7, Hoarding Flower I–III and chapter nine, Telling my Story, helped you make sense of how your beliefs, emotions and behaviours interplay. Telling my Story helped you make connections with your past experiences which may have contributed to the beliefs that you hold in relation to your hoarding. You may have found that it also helped to answer some of your questions about how the condition developed. The knowledge is useful but it does not bring about change. We can all look into our past and identify specific situations or points that have affected us either negatively or positively. But we do not have the ability to go back into the past to change what has happened. So the important thing to remember is that these experiences and beliefs are affecting us now. We can review the past to help us to move on and work on the present.

Here we will look at working with your beliefs. These beliefs are powerful as they govern the way you feel about and respond to situations. For example, you may have a belief that, 'My photographs are a link to my past'. Therefore photographs are significant for you. In the event that your photographs are damaged or destroyed, you may feel distressed and be hard on yourself for not taking more care of them. You can see from this example how you may be affected emotionally and behaviourally by losing your photographs.

It is therefore very important to address beliefs that play an active role in maintaining hoarding. But remember that beliefs are not bad – they serve a function. The impact they make is shaped by whether we hold them rigidly or with flexibility. If our beliefs are held rigidly, they tend to have a negative effect on us. If we develop a way to be flexible in how we view situations it will make it easier to cope and deal with them. The skills that you learn in this book can be applied to other areas of your life. This is the nature of CBT – it is flexible and can be applied to many challenges.

Understanding your beliefs

Our beliefs are active all the time. The key thing is to recognise when your beliefs are having an effect. A tip for helping you spot this is to notice when you are experiencing uncomfortable feelings, indicating that your beliefs about a situation have been activated and your interpretation of the situation (based on your beliefs) is causing you to feel the way you do. For example, you may hold a belief that everything you own is important and when you are decluttering you may feel uncomfortable. This is because you have interpreted what you are doing as getting rid of things that are of value and importance to you. It may be helpful to start becoming aware of these uncomfortable feelings. Start by accepting the way you are feeling and ask yourself some of these useful questions to help identify your beliefs:

What does this feeling mean to me?

What are the reasons why I am feeling this way?

Additionally, you can try to connect with the feeling that you are experiencing as a means to help you identify your beliefs. Ask yourself, Where am I experiencing this feeling in my body?

Place your hand where you are experiencing this feeling.

Connect with this feeling.

Is any colour associated with it?

Ask yourself, When was the very first time that I remember feeling this feeling?

Describe the memory that you experience.

Ask yourself, What does this memory mean to me?

What does the memory say about me?

List your beliefs and assumptions. In your hoarding flower formulation we discussed how to identify these by writing them down as 'if . . . then . . . ' statements (see p. 97). 'If . . . .then . . . ' statements are useful as it will be easier to challenge them.

My belief is:

I am ....

....

....

If ....

....

....

Then ....

....

....

Now having identified the beliefs and assumptions, we need to start working on them.

The basic technique for working on your beliefs is to dispute them. In this way we can identify the way we interpret a situation and assess the evidence for and against the belief.

Often we tend to interpret information or situations based on the way we feel. Our emotions can distort the reality of the situation. For example, if you are angry, you often look at evidence to support the reasons why you are angry rather than understanding the situation fully.

To help you make sense of these distortions, we look at the notion of unhelpful thinking patterns below. Everyone engages in unhelpful thinking patterns – it is common – but recognising them helps you view things differently.

Black-and-white thinking

This involves viewing things in a concrete way. In this way there are no grey or in-between areas. Things are either good or bad. Black-and-white thinking is inflexible and rigid and leads us to a global view in the same way. This thinking does not allow any room to consider other perspectives. Let's look at the example of a rainy day. We could say that the day is wet and it is bad (black and white) or we could consider that it is wet, the temperature is mild and the garden is getting watered, leaving the situation not as negative as we originally considered it.

Labelling

The labelling of yourself, others or a situation in a negative way. For example, I am useless, they are bad, the place is a tip. Labelling is not helpful because when we apply labels we tend to behave in a manner that supports our badge. For example, you might view your own environment as being beyond help. You may have labelled it as such and therefore it is highly unlikely that you are going to try and sort the place out.

Mental filtering

Mental filtering happens when you disregard the positive around you. An example would be if you had worked hard on de-cluttering your environment but then you choose to ignore all the work and focus instead on the areas that you have not worked on. Another example could be remembering all the things that have not gone as well as planned during the day. Mental filtering affects you – it is demotivating and effectively blanks out all the good work.

Disqualifying the positive

Disqualifying the positive means not recognising the good or positive aspects of the situation. For example: you have cleared out a section of your room but when asked about what you have done in your environment, you say, 'I have not done much.' Consider the impact of not recognising what you have done; you are likely to feel disheartened and less motivated.

Mind reading

We believe we know what other people are thinking about us or how they will react to us. For example, if you are considering telling your close friends or family about your hoarding problem, you might have thoughts that they are going to react in a negative way and, as a result, you do not tell them and do not receive the support that could be offered. In reality, it is often the case that others do not react in the way we think that they are going to.

Emotional reasoning

When we use our feelings as evidence of a situation we are emotionally reasoning. In preparing to de-clutter your space you might say, 'I do not feel that I can do it' and, as a result, you do not even try. You never know whether you are able or unable to clear your space without trying it out first. We often use emotional reasoning and it prevents us from finding out the reality of the situation.

Catastrophising

We leap straight to thinking about a catastrophe when we picture the worst-case scenario. For example, imagine you allow a friend or family member to help and you jump to the conclusion that they will disrupt everything and throw away your belongings without your knowledge. Another example of this is when you decide to throw away some old newspapers and you worry that you might need them in the future. This leads you to feel anxious. Jumping to conclusions tends to affect you by making you feel anxious and worry excessively.

Demands

You have high standards and expectations for yourself or others. These demands affect you as they are rigid and hard to meet. For example, when de-cluttering your space, if you have an expectation that you will clear a certain amount and then fail to reach that expectation, it can lead you to feel demotivated and experience negative emotions. Making your demands more adaptive and flexible will encourage you to progress.

Overgeneralisation

Overgeneralisation occurs when you take one situation and apply it to be something that would occur all the time. If you have arranged for a friend to help you with your de-cluttering and you receive a message that they are not able to meet you that day, you feel let down. You may have the opportunity to reorganise your friend's visit, but not when you jump to the conclusion that they will let you down again just because it has happened once before. Another example could be that you clear your space, gradually fill it with more items again and feel that because you have had one setback then nothing is ever going to change. This will lead you to feel demotivated and give up.

Blame, or personalisation

When you feel that something is your fault, you are personalising. For example, you may feel it is your fault that your space has become cluttered. Blame or personalisation is not helpful as it prevents you developing the compassionate understanding of your problem that would be more helpful.

Fortune telling

You may feel that you know how things are going to turn out. If you are getting a friend to help you with the de-cluttering, you predict that they are going to throw everything out and you will have no control. The result is that you experience negative emotions and feel that you are not able to cope, preventing you from doing the work you had intended to do. Fortune telling is forecasting how things are going to be without experience.

Low frustration tolerance

You hide from uncomfortable feelings when you have low frustration tolerance. For example, when de-cluttering you might experience negative feelings and, as a result, you avoid feeling this way by engaging with other activities that are not related to your hoarding. Or you might experience negative emotions when attempting to discard items you have saved and this could result in you continuing to save them as a way of coping with those feelings. Low frustration tolerance leads you to avoid engaging with your hoarding issues.

Identify your thought patterns

Having gone through the various unhelpful thinking patterns, we will now see how they overlap with each other. The first step is to identify your collection of patterns. Let's imagine you have identified your belief as, 'I am vulnerable.' The patterns connected with this could include:

Black-and-white thinking.

Labelling (identifying as vulnerable).

Mental filtering.

Disqualifying the positive.

Catastrophising.

Emotional reasoning.

Fortune telling.

You will notice that there are a number of unhelpful thinking patterns involved in your belief. The next step is to challenge it. As discussed earlier in this chapter, you need to write down the evidence which proves or disproves your belief.

My belief is: I am vulnerable.

Evidence for	Evidence against

Having written down this evidence it is now important to review it. Check if the evidence is concrete, based on fact and is not influenced by your unhelpful thinking patterns. These patterns fuel our negative emotions and unhelpful behaviours. Reviewing the evidence for and against your belief will help you to have a more balanced view and to deal with your beliefs. Unhelpful thinking patterns negate positive aspects leading to your negative beliefs being supported. But after reviewing the evidence you may reach a more balanced conclusion, for example, 'I am capable in some aspects and vulnerable in some others.' This view is less rigid and allows you to focus on the areas in which you are capable and develop ways of dealing with the areas in which you are less so.

Sometimes you may find it difficult to challenge your beliefs. Sometimes we find it easier to help others than we do dealing with our own problems. Here are some helpful suggestions to help yourself when you are experiencing a difficulty:

What would you say to a friend who believed that he/she was vulnerable?

If you were to tell a friend that you believed that you were vulnerable, what would the friend say to you?

Try strengthening your new, more balanced belief by keeping a written positive data log to support it. Write it down and review it at the end of each day.

Addressing your beliefs

Having discussed working on your beliefs, it is important to try dealing with them. A good way to begin is to become aware of which emotions feel uncomfortable. As previously discussed, these uncomfortable emotions indicate that your beliefs have been activated, so recognising them is a good starting point. Work in a step-by-step manner (as discussed above) to identify your beliefs, and write them down.

My beliefs are:

....

....

....

....

....

....

....

....

....

....

....

....

....

Questioning and beliefs

Next, recognise the unhelpful thinking patterns:

Belief	Unhelpful thinking patterns

The evidence supporting and disproving my beliefs is:

Evidence for	Evidence against

Having reviewed the evidence for and against my beliefs, my balanced beliefs are:

....

....

....

....

....

....

....

....

Keep a daily log of positive experiences that support your balanced belief and review it at the end of each day.

Family and friends

Identifying and challenging beliefs is difficult. If your support is accepted you can play a very helpful role in asking questions to help identify beliefs and also in providing alternative perspectives. When looking for evidence for and against beliefs, we all have a tendency to miss possible alternatives, so helping someone to identify other ways of thinking about the belief can be invaluable. Take the lead from the person you are supporting. When they have developed more helpful alternative beliefs, encouraging your friend or family member to keep a positive data log will help to reinforce these new beliefs. It is hard work and focusing on their initial vision can serve to remind why the person is working on their hoarding issues. It may be that suggesting a rewarding activity afterwards helps them to recognise the progress they are making.

Tips

- Become more in tune with the way you feel, as it will help you to identify your beliefs.
- Use the techniques discussed above to help develop your skills at reframing your beliefs.
- Be consistent – do not take shortcuts as it is worth investing the time in dealing with your beliefs. Your negative beliefs and assumptions perpetuate your problem.
- If you are stuck, ask a friend or family member to help you to identify and challenge your beliefs.
- Practise recognising the unhelpful thinking patterns daily – on your own and in your interactions with others.
- Always acknowledge the way you are feeling. This will help with your tolerance of uncomfortable feelings.

- Do not be afraid to question the way you are feeling. It will help you understand why you are feeling that way.
- Extend your limits of discomfort. It will help you develop your level of tolerance and cope better in the longer term.
- The more you practise, the easier it will become.

Obstacles

'I am finding it too difficult to identify my beliefs.'

Do not worry excessively about getting it right. The important thing is to practise the techniques and, where possible, ask a friend or family member to help you. The most important thing is to make a link with the uncomfortable feeling and check out what it means to you.

'I can't find the evidence for and against my beliefs.'

Sometimes it is difficult to identify the evidence. Try stepping back and imagine that you are helping a friend. Often it is easier helping someone else as you have emotional distance.

'It is time consuming.'

Yes, it is time consuming, but the benefits will be long-term. The more you work on them, the more practiced you will become and the easier this will be in the long run.

Key messages

- Everyone has both positive and negative beliefs, but

when these beliefs are rigidly held, they become unhelpful.

- Some unhelpful beliefs perpetuate your difficulties.
- It is important to work on and address your beliefs as they affect the way you feel and react (behaviourally) to situations.
- We cannot change the past; however we can revisit the past and understand it differently.
- Use your vision to help you keep focused in dealing with your hoarding issues.

15

Go with the flow – staying with feelings

De-cluttering alone will not solve your issues with hoarding. It is useful to address the beliefs associated with your hoarding. You will have identified beliefs in chapters 5–7 Hoarding Flower I–III and in the previous chapter. The aim now is to work on the beliefs that maintain your hoarding.

Each of us experiences emotions or feelings and we all develop our own way of dealing with these. It is normal to experience both positive and negative emotions and find uncomfortable emotions difficult to deal with. We engage in a range of behaviours to help us cope with these feelings. Some of this behaviour is helpful and some is not. For example, if you have a fear of dogs and feel anxious when you see one, you might avoid areas where you might most likely come across dogs, such as parks. Avoiding dogs is helpful in the short term, but in the long term it is unhelpful and limiting as you are not able to spend time in parks.

It is important to consider how to address your own uncomfortable feelings so that you can deal with your issues effectively. In part one, we discussed the Cognitive Behavioural Therapy (CBT) model and how our thoughts influence the way we feel. The emotions that we experience are essentially a result of how we interpret situations. In the example above, when you see a dog your immediate appraisal of the situation might be, 'The dog is coming near me . . . it is going to jump on me . . . it might bite me'. This appraisal will result in you feeling anxious and will probably leave you wanting to avoid the situation.

Similarly, when you see a room filled with things you may end up feeling overwhelmed by the situation. You may conclude that you are not able to cope and avoid thinking about or dealing with what you need to do, leading to the environment becoming more cluttered and you losing more space.

In the chapters on your hoarding flower you identified some of the uncomfortable feelings and emotions that you experience. It is now helpful to start considering the subtle behaviours that are associated with the experience of these emotions. The subtle behaviours maintain and perpetuate these feelings.

Address your uncomfortable feelings

There are many ways to start addressing the uncomfortable feelings. The first step is to recognise them and acknowledge that you feel this way. It does not matter whether you have a name for these feelings or not – what is important is how they are affecting you. A common behaviour associated with feelings is to ignore them – If I do not think about them, I will be fine.

Firstly, acknowledge these feelings by accepting them. For example: I am feeling this discomfort in my stomach; I am feeling anxious at this moment. It is OK to feel this way. Accepting your feelings will enable you to face them and help you to deal with them. The reason feelings are uncomfortable is partly because of how we view them and this is related to our unhelpful thinking patterns. For example, thinking, I can't cope with feeling this way suggests black-and-white thinking (you can either cope or not at all), mental filtering (not recognising the times when you have coped and managed), demands (feeling that you *should* be able to cope), and low frustration tolerance (running away from feelings by engaging in behaviour that is not helpful). As discussed in chapter thirteen, these patterns can also take the form of self-talk where we talk ourselves into feeling far more distress than we originally experienced.

Often, when we experience uncomfortable emotions we believe that feeling them is bad for us. For example, some people who experience high levels of anxiety believe that the anxiety is going to kill them. Our past experiences of these uncomfortable feelings often lead us to engage in behaviour such as avoidance as a means to escape the way we are feeling. When feelings are uncomfortable, the immediate response is to find a way to end the discomfort we are experiencing. The more we try to run away from these emotions, the lower our ability to tolerate these feelings. For example, imagine it is a very hot day and you are outdoors. There is nothing you can do to avoid feeling the heat, but you will notice that the longer you stay in the environment, the less hot you feel. This is because you have accepted that it is hot and there is nothing you can actually do about it. You disengage from self-talk about how hot it is and remain in the environment until you have become acclimatised.

As we deal with uncomfortable feelings, we will use all the techniques discussed above. You may have noticed as you have progressed through this book how our thoughts, emotions and behaviours impact on each other. Working with your uncomfortable feelings will help you develop your skills further in dealing with your beliefs, emotions and unhelpful behaviours.

Physical responses to feelings

The next step is to recognise that you are experiencing uncomfortable feelings. As with the other exercises, it may be helpful to start by picking up items you intend to sort out or discard. Be aware of any changes in the way you feel and notice any changes in your bodily sensations, such as the following:

- An increase in your heart rate.
- Feeling shaky, hot and sweaty.
- Butterflies in your stomach.

It may be helpful for you to name these feelings as it will be easier for you to recognise them in the future. Ask yourself:

Go with the flow – staying with feelings

What is this feeling I am feeling right now?

....
....
....
....
....
....
....
....

What does this feeling mean to me?

....
....
....
....
....
....
....
....

What am I saying to myself (self-talk) when I feel this way?

....

....

....

....

....

....

....

....

How do I see the situation? What are my unhelpful thinking patterns?

....

....

....

....

....

....

....

....

Go with the flow – staying with feelings

How much attention am I giving to these feelings?

....
....
....
....
....
....
....

What am I doing to make these feelings stay a long time? What are the behaviours that I am engaging in (such as focusing on the bodily symptoms or trying to get rid of the feelings)?

....
....
....
....
....
....
....

What am I doing to cope with these feelings? What are the behaviours that I engage in to cope with these feelings, such as avoidance or talking about them, etc?

....

....

....

....

....

....

....

....

The next step is to try to understand the way in which self-talk and behaviour keep these feelings going. When I feel:

....

....

....

....

....

....

....

.... my thoughts are:

....

....

....

....

....,

....

....

....

When considering my thoughts, my unhelpful thinking patterns are:

....

....

....

....

....

....

....

How helpful is it for me to view the situation in this way and what impact does it have on my uncomfortable feelings?

....

....

....

....

....

....

....

....

Now that you have recognised and become aware of your uncomfortable feelings, your thinking and your behaviours, you can address the emotions. Recognise that it is normal to experience uncomfortable feelings. You are dealing with an area of your life that you find difficult, such as sorting out and discarding items that have significance. It is perfectly normal for that to cause you discomfort. Learn to be kind to yourself. Take a compassionate view of the way you are feeling. For example, you might say, 'I have to sort and discard some of the things that I value and treasure and I am experiencing uncomfortable feelings, distress and upset. It is normal to feel this way. Anyone who has to deal with a similar situation will experience similar feelings to me. Feelings are normal and it is OK to feel the way I feel.'

Developing a compassionate understanding of the uncomfortable feelings will help you to accept the way you feel at that moment. We often have high expectations, standards or demands about the way we feel. For example, 'must not show my emotions'. By being kinder, we accept the fact that we will experience these emotions – it is OK to have them – and we will be more likely to tolerate them.

My compassionate view of the uncomfortable emotions that I am feeling is:

....

....

....

....

....

....

....

....

....

....

....

....

....

....

....

....

....

....

....

The next step is to distance yourself from your uncomfortable feelings. This does not mean avoiding these feelings. By trying to avoid them, you would probably engage in unhelpful behaviour. In this case, distancing means reducing your focus on these feelings by reducing the attention you give to them. One example of selective attention is constant monitoring of the way you are feeling.

Let's try a simple experiment. Firstly, try to experience some negative emotions – consider discarding one of the items you hoard. Rate the strength of the feeling on a scale of one to ten, one being mild (comfortable) and ten being the strongest (most uncomfortable).

The emotion that I am feeling is: _____

The strength of the emotion at this moment is ____ out of ten.

Now, focus again on the emotion and what do you notice?

The strength of the emotion at this moment is ___ out of ten.

What did you notice? Did you find that the intensity of the emotion became higher? If so, that is because you have given the negative emotion prominence by focusing on it. In addition, you would have probably engaged in some self-talk about the way you are feeling which only perpetuates that feeling.

One of the best ways to deal with negative emotions is to learn to stay with the feeling by acknowledging it and not engaging with the way you feel. We appreciate that this is difficult, but with practice it becomes easier. Some people cope by keeping busy, as this distracts you from the way you are feeling, but in reality this only keeps the feelings going. Distraction is a form of avoidance which is not helpful. The aim is to develop a more adaptive and helpful coping mechanism.

One way of dealing with these negative emotions is by not engaging with them for a short period of time at first and then gradually increasing the time. It is helpful to start at a level that you feel that you can cope with, for example, not engaging for two minutes, and gradually build it up to ten minutes or longer. A common misconception is that you cannot cope with these feelings. By gradually increasing the time you tolerate them for, you will be able to challenge your belief that you are not able to cope with uncomfortable feelings.

Another intervention is mindfulness. Mindfulness is a form of meditation that originates from the Zen Buddhist tradition. It is not a religious practice – mindfulness meditations are based on the principles of non-engagement and acceptance. Please remember, mindfulness is not about relaxing. Mindfulness means essentially being in the moment and not judging or comparing. We often tend to compare how we feel from moment to moment. When we are mindful, we are aware of the uncomfortable emotions, without judging or comparing with the past or considering what it will feel like in the future. Mindfulness is practised by everyone on a daily basis but is not recognised. Let's return to the example of experiencing a hot day when there is nothing you can do to change that. If you accept that it is a hot day (being in the moment) and let it be, you will find that you are able to cope and deal with it better. On the other hand, if you engage with the fact that it is a hot day – 'I cannot cope, it was not as hot as this yesterday' – you will find that you feel the heat more acutely as your engagement is affecting the way you react to the situation.

Make a list to help you recognise some of the other daily activities in which you do not engage in self-talk or selective attention and which have principles of mindfulness (being in the moment and not judging). Examples may include eating, cleaning your teeth or cooking:

....

....

....

....

....

....

....

....

Here is a simple mindfulness exercise that you can practise on a daily basis. This exercise will only take ten minutes
and you may wish to gradually extend the length of time of
the exercise. Read the instructions first and become familiar
with them. If you want to, you can record the instructions
or ask a friend or family member to read them out to you.

Find a time of the day when you would be least disturbed
by noise or by another person. Honour yourself as a person
by making time for yourself and engaging in activities that
will help you progress in life. Make this time your time. Sit
on a comfortable chair and close your eyes if you wish.

Start your mindfulness exercise by focusing on your
breath.

There is no need to breathe deeply, just breathe in and
out normally.

Have a non-judgemental awareness of the breath coming
in and out.

Be aware of the place where you are. If you are sitting,
be aware of the position you are sitting in and your body's

physical contact with the chair or floor. Again, remember it is a non-judgemental awareness.

Be aware of the sounds in your environment. There is no need to label them or describe what they are.

If you notice that your mind is engaging with your thoughts, bring your attention back to your breath. Focus again on it going in and out.

If your mind starts wandering, gently remind yourself that it has done so. Accept it and let it go by bringing your attention back to your breathing until you have finished the exercise.

The same principles can be applied to your uncomfortable feelings. Once you become aware of them, let them be there but there is no need to engage with them. Do not create a narrative about what it feels like, what it felt like earlier or what it might feel like later. Just stay with the feeling and let it be there.

Practise these simple exercises and you will find that, over time, you develop a higher tolerance of uncomfortable feelings. You can transfer these techniques to other areas of your life, especially when you find that you are ruminating about items that have been discarded.

Remember that these uncomfortable feelings are familiar as you experience them regularly. When feelings are uncomfortable, people often feel that they are experiencing them for the first time. But you can accept and normalise these emotions by inviting them in and treating them as old familiar friends. By doing so, you can change your beliefs and your attitudes towards them, making them less threatening and more acceptable.

When you experience these uncomfortable feelings, respond with:

'These are old familiar friends, I know them well.'

'Hello, old friends, welcome in – I am not going to fight with you.'

You will find the more you treat these feelings in this way, the easier they are to manage and the faster they are to fade. Practise experiencing these feelings and welcoming them – notice the difference in the way you feel and deal with them.

Family and friends

We all experience uncomfortable emotions and it is generally helpful for us to acknowledge and tolerate these feelings rather than to avoid them. Talking about our own emotions in an appropriate way can help to normalise them. You may also act as a role model, demonstrating adaptive ways of coping. Being there and understanding the concepts explained in this chapter may be invaluable to the person you are supporting. Many of us have a tendency to busy ourselves to avoid or distract from difficult emotions. Naming this avoidance is a step towards addressing it. Letting your friend or family member know that you are there and can help if they encounter difficulties in sitting with the emotions can give them security and help facilitate changes. If you would like to, engage in the mindfulness exercises. Sharing and discussing your experiences may be enriching for you both.

Tips

- Identify the coping mechanisms that you use with your uncomfortable feelings, as some of them can be unhelpful and maintain and perpetuate those feelings.
- Gradually drop your coping mechanisms and replace them with more adaptive mechanisms such as not avoiding the feelings and distracting from them.
- Be consistent in learning to tolerate your uncomfortable feelings.
- If you are stuck, ask a friend or family member to support you in tolerating the feelings.
- As you learn to recognise and accept your uncomfortable feelings, you will begin to challenge your beliefs and change your coping mechanisms.
- Practise mindfulness regularly to help with being in the moment and developing a different relationship with your feelings.
- Always acknowledge the way you are feeling. This will help with your tolerance of uncomfortable feelings.
- Do not be afraid to question the way you are feeling – it will help you to understand the reasons you feel this way.
- Accept and welcome your uncomfortable feelings. Do not avoid the way you feel.
- The more you accept and learn to stay with your uncomfortable feelings, the less distressing they will be.

Obstacles

'I am finding it too difficult to identify my uncomfortable feelings.'

Do not worry about having a name for the feelings that you experience. The key thing is recognising them and learning to accept that that is how you are feeling at this moment.

'I am finding it hard to tolerate my uncomfortable feelings.'

Accept that the feelings are uncomfortable and identify the behaviour that maintains and perpetuates these feelings. This behaviour may be temporarily helpful but in the long term keeps the uncomfortable feelings going. Learn to welcome and tolerate these feelings and it will become easier. Use the techniques discussed above to help you with tolerating.

'I need to focus on clearing out my space.'

Dealing with your emotions is part and parcel of reclaiming your space. Clearing out alone is not going to help with your hoarding issues as you need to deal with the underlying factors that drive them. Uncomfortable emotions are one of the driving factors. When you deal with these emotions you are also working on the other maintaining factors such as your beliefs and behaviours.

Key messages

- Emotions are a normal human experience. People do not like uncomfortable emotions and often find ways of dealing with them.
- Some coping mechanisms are not helpful as they perpetuate uncomfortable emotions.

- Avoiding uncomfortable emotions is not helpful. Welcoming them will help you develop your level of tolerance.
- Remember that short-term discomfort has long-term gains.
- Use your original vision and image from chapter two to help you keep focussed in dealing with your hoarding.
- Recognise the space you have reclaimed so far.

16

Round and round
– rumination

Rumination can mean different things to different people. In terms of hoarding, rumination simply means worrying, thinking, recalling and playing back events or situations associated with your items in your mind while you de-clutter. It is important to remember that rumination is a normal and natural occurrence. Each and every one of us deals with rumination differently. However, the consequences of engaging in rumination are often negative as it can cause us great distress; it is time-consuming and can paralyse an individual. In relation to your hoarding behaviour, engaging in rumination can often lead you to hoard more. You may have experienced rumination on your journey to reclaim your space, as you de-clutter.

We assume rumination serves a function in helping us to feel better, but in fact it has the opposite effect. You will notice that rumination has both a cognitive (thought-based) and a behavioural element. We ruminate as a means of coping with the uncomfortable feelings that we experience. We try to reduce the gap between the distress we are feeling and how we would like to feel. The more we engage with our rumination, the more we discover that it is never-ending. It is negative and unhelpful and it maintains our unhelpful beliefs and feelings and contributes to our hoarding problems.

It is always useful to refer back to your formulation of the hoarding flower in chapters 5–7 as it helps make the links between your thoughts, feelings and behaviours. You will notice how these three components interplay and maintain your hoarding problems. For example:

The degree of mental energy spent on ruminating is far greater than that expected on dealing with your hoarding issues. Rumination fuels your doubts and erodes your confidence in the decisions you make about sorting and de-cluttering. When you have these doubts, you seek more reassurance, which leads to even more doubts and engaging in more rumination with the hope of gaining certainty. Remember, we are never able to gain a hundred per cent certainty about anything that we do. One hundred per cent certainty is rigid – black-and-white thinking – and the key consideration should be to be flexible and learn to accept the situation as it is.

Flexibility is one of the key tools for dealing with your hoarding. Being flexible enables you to let things go with greater ease – it will help with accepting that some things have to go and behaviour has to change in order for you to be able to reclaim your space and your life. Keep your chapter two vision in mind to remind you as to where you wish to be in terms of your hoarding issues. You would have found advice in each of the previous chapters in this part of the book to help you develop flexibility in your approach to dealing with your hoarding.

Recognise rumination

Rumination is intrusive and emotion-laden. Often, when you are trying to cope with uncomfortable feelings, you engage in rumination as a means of coping with these feelings. Rumination only provides temporary relief and is not long-lasting. In the previous chapter, we discussed alternative ways to cope with these feelings. You may have noticed that the same feelings come back. This is because rumination is not an effective way to deal with your uncomfortable feelings.

Develop your own formulation of your rumination using the hoarding flower:

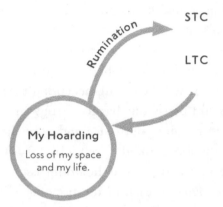

Once you recognise that you are engaging in ruminative behaviour and understand how it contributes to your hoarding, the next step is to acknowledge you are ruminating. People rarely acknowledge what they are doing or what is happening to them. Once you have acknowledged that you are engaging in ruminative behaviour you can start working on it. One of the techniques we discussed in the previous chapter was staying with your feelings. This same technique also applies to rumination. Staying with your rumination means not engaging with it. Not engaging means being aware of the rumination but not having a dialogue. Dialogue is a process of engagement in which you are trying to deal with or solve the doubt you may have but may in fact open up further doubts.

It is understandable that at the beginning staying with the rumination is difficult. Start by staying with it for two minutes without engaging and then gradually increase the length of time. Like all the exercises in this book, it is an activity you will need to practise. It is important to be consistent in your approach to dealing with rumination.

We discussed mindfulness in the previous chapter. Mindfulness is about being in the moment and being non-judgemental. Being judgemental means you are engaging and evaluating the situation. Mindfulness shouldn't be confused with distraction. Distraction is an act to deliberately avoid a thought, feeling or behaviour. However, in mindfulness you are aware of that thought, feeling or behaviour but you are not reacting to it.

Learning to welcome the intrusion as you did with your uncomfortable feelings is a good way of learning to accept it. By welcoming it you are removing the significance you place on it. It will be less distressing and easier to tolerate. Developing a welcoming attitude is a skill that can be used in all areas of your life – you will find that when you welcome an area that is perceived as difficult, you experience less resistance and it becomes easier to deal with. In addition, being welcoming deals with your expectations. When we have a certain expectation which is not met, it triggers a downward spiral of searching and questioning that is part of the ruminative process of trying to understand and make yourself feel better.

Practise, on a daily basis, welcoming a difficulty such as a feeling or task. Find out how it feels to be welcoming and how you manage it. It will be a journey of discovery as you will learn something new about this process.

223

Recognising intrusions

The next step is to recognise when a thought pops into your head that makes you feel uncomfortable and leads you to engage in ruminative behaviour, going round and round trying to find answers and make yourself feel better. When you notice this has happened, say to yourself:

I have just had an intrusive thought or doubt pop into my head. My immediate reaction is:

....

....

....

....

....

....

....

....

....

As a result of this thought popping into my head, what am I feeling?

....

....

....
....
....
....
....
....
....
....

How am I dealing with this feeling? What are the things I am doing in my head to cope with this feeling?

....
....
....
....
....
....
....
....
....

Now normalise the thought to help you understand that it isn't unusual to feel this way. Most people who experience intrusive thoughts will feel this way.

It is normal to have these thoughts of..............................

....

....

....

....

....

....

.... that lead me to engage with them, making them more significant.

Normalising these thoughts will help you accept that the doubts that you experience keep the uncomfortable feelings going. Welcome the thoughts as they are frequent visitors to your mind. You know them well and they are familiar.

Next, learn to stay with the thought and the feeling. This happens by not engaging with them. Try not to monitor the way you are feeling. Try not to comment or engage in self-talk about the way you are feeling. Begin by just staying with the thoughts and feelings for two minutes and gradually increase the length of time. What do you notice when you stay with the thoughts and feelings?

When I stay with the thoughts I notice:

....

....

....

....

....

....

....

....

As I increase the amount of time without engaging I notice:

....

....

....

....

....

....

....

....

By not engaging with this thought I have noticed:

....

....

....

....

....

....

....

....

Not engaging with the intrusive thoughts was helpful because I:

....

....

....

....

....

....

....

....

What was unhelpful and led to me engaging more with my intrusive thoughts was:

....

....

....

....

....

....

....

....

Welcome your intrusive thoughts and doubts. Make it a daily habit to welcome your intrusive thoughts and let them be there – Hello, old friends, you are welcome to visit me. You are familiar old friends and you are always welcome.

By welcoming the intrusive thoughts that lead to your ruminative behaviour you are reducing their significance and they will gradually become something of little or no importance.

You can also use the mindfulness technique we discussed in the previous chapter to deal with your rumination by staying in the moment. In doing so, you are not comparing things or judging how they were or how they are going to be. Being in the moment will help you accept thoughts as just thoughts and there will be no need to engage with them.

Bring your intrusive thoughts to mind and let them be there; there is no need to judge or comment on them. Be aware of what is around you. Be aware of how it is without judging or engaging with it.

Another mindfulness technique that is quick and easy to use is the mindfulness of sound. This aural exercise is about hearing and not listening, which is quite different. When we listen, we are deliberately tuning into something specific such as a speaker; when we are hearing, we absorb everything around us rather than one specific sound.

Here is a simple exercise involving the mindfulness of sound. It is short and easy to follow. Read it over a few times until it is familiar enough and you can easily practise it without having to refer to the book. Carry out the exercise for short periods of time at first. You might want to start with five minutes and gradually increase the length.

Start your mindfulness exercise with a focus on your breath.

There is no need to breathe deeply, just use your normal breathing in and out.

Have a non-judgemental awareness of the breath coming in and out.

Be aware of your surroundings and, if in a sitting position, the contact of the chair or floor with your body. Again, remember to have a non-judgemental awareness.

Be aware of your surroundings and the sounds in your environment – there is no need to label or describe them.

If you notice that your mind is engaging with your thoughts, bring your attention back to your breathing and the moment of going in and going out. Be gentle with yourself and accept that your mind has started to engage but that is OK.

Bring your awareness back to your environment and to the sounds that may be present.

Develop your own mindfulness techniques – whatever you find helpful that works for you. Mindfulness can be practised anywhere or with any activity. The key principles are to be in the moment, not to be judgemental, to stay with thoughts or feelings – leaving them as they are – and not to judge your feelings for what they were, are or will mean to you. There is no comparison with the way your life was, how it is and how it will be. Do not forget you have the resources to deal with your intrusive thoughts, doubts, difficulties and challenges.

You will notice throughout this book how exercises in each chapter are used to deal with other difficulties. All the techniques discussed can be used across all the challenges you face. Follow them as it also helps you become familiar with them and develop your skills.

Family and friends

So that we can best support our friend or family member we need to look after ourselves. It may be hard for us to live with the clutter and the consequences of another's hoarding behaviour that, in some cases, will seem over-whelming and difficult to address. We all ruminate and go over thoughts in our minds. One way of making it easier to be with the person who has hoarding issues is to work on our own wellbeing and use some of the ways described above to help manage our own worries, fears and nega-tive thoughts. You may like to try to acknowledge and stay with your own rumination while not engaging with the thoughts. Note what happens for you. The mindfulness of sounds exercise can work for all, so have a go and spend more time in the here and now. Sometimes, sharing any difficulties you encounter may help bring closeness and solidarity in your relationship with the person you are supporting. Others may find this very personal and, if so, respect the boundaries of privacy. You might also like to take a moment to think about how else you could look after your own needs and wellbeing.

Tips

- Be aware of intrusive thoughts or doubts that you experience. They are automatic and have uncomfortable feelings that come with them.
- Deliberately bring intrusive thoughts to the front of your mind. Do not avoid them. Avoiding them makes them significant.
- Identify ruminative, round-and-round behaviour.

- Recognise the ruminative pattern and what leads you to engage with it.
- Develop an attitude of welcoming towards these thoughts and associated feelings.
- Practise mindfulness regularly to help with being in the moment and to develop a different relationship with your intrusive thoughts and doubts.
- It is normal to have thoughts and feelings.
- Accept that intrusive thoughts are normal. Try not to avoid them.
- Develop an attitude of acceptance. Accept the way you feel right in the moment. There is no need to compare to the past or worry about the future.
- Make mindfulness a part of your life and use it in all activities that you undertake.
- Develop an attitude of flexibility and apply this to everything that you do.

Obstacles

'My intrusive thoughts or doubts are too strong.'

Yes, the thoughts might feel very strong and the feelings can be uncomfortable. One reason they are strong is the significance you have given them. Learn to stay with them without engaging for short periods of time and gradually increase the length of time you do this. Remind yourself to accept that they are only thoughts.

'I am finding it hard to tolerate the feelings that come with my thoughts.'

Yes, often our thoughts come with feelings that can be uncomfortable. Accept that the feelings are uncomfortable. Learn to stay with them for short periods of time without interacting with them; use your mindfulness techniques to help both with your thoughts and feelings. They will pass.

'The mindfulness exercises are hard.'

The mindfulness exercises appear to be hard as you are learning and developing a skill that you are not familiar with. Mindfulness is helping you to change the way you relate to your thoughts, feelings and, gradually, other areas of your life. Practise it in all your activities. You will find that it will become easier and a way of life for you.

Key messages

- Ruminations are linked to both your thoughts and behaviour.
- Identify the patterns of coping that are associated with your intrusive thoughts, doubts and uncomfortable feelings.
- Remember that questioning or discussing your intrusive thoughts or doubts are forms of engagement.
- Engaging with intrusive thoughts will only serve to make them significant and more emotionally distressing.
- Mindfulness is helpful in developing an attitude of being in the moment, non-judgemental and accepting.
- Writing down helpful and unhelpful behaviour as a

record which will assist you when you are dealing with your rumination.

- These techniques can be used to deal with your thoughts, feelings and behaviour.
- Focus on your vision and review how far you have come.

17

To do or not to do
– procrastination

In the previous chapter, we talked about rumination and how to address it. Another important area that needs attention is procrastination. Procrastination is a common unhelpful behaviour that people with hoarding and other disorders engage in. Procrastination is debilitating; when people engage in this behaviour it stops them from doing the activities that they had intended.

When people engage in procrastination, it often leads them to experience uncomfortable feelings. One of the reasons they have these uncomfortable feelings is that for them things have to be done in a certain way. When they are not able to do them as planned, they focus on the uncomfortable feelings which prevented them instead. Often, people complain that they have not done anything productive all day as they were trying to ensure that everything was in place first before they started dealing with their hoarding issues.

Procrastination is not dissimilar to rumination but is often driven by the need or belief to have things right or, at least, to feel right. Like rumination, procrastination is a trap that people fall into and is counterproductive to their intention or vision. It is a behaviour that is counterproductive and does not lead to the completion of tasks.

Procrastination is dictated by conditions or standards we impose on ourselves. When these conditions or standards are not met, we do not feel able to progress and remain stuck and it becomes an obstacle. For example, in trying to ensure that items are placed in the appropriate recycling bins, we might get stuck in an internal debate about which item needs to go into which bin.

It is important to identify this behaviour. Often people can get so engaged with procrastination that they are not aware they are doing it. One of its key features is self-talk. As discussed in chapter thirteen, self-talk is an internal dialogue that people have when making a decision.

For example, when throwing unwanted items away, the dialogue might be as follows:

D1: I need to throw it out.

D2: Shall I take the step of throwing it out?

D1: I'm not sure I am ready.

D2: I need to do it.

D1: Maybe later I can try.

D2: But I need to throw things out...

You can see the debate that takes places when someone is procrastinating – and this can go on for hours without coming to a decision or resolution.

You will notice that, while rumination and procrastination are similar, the difference is that ruminating is characterised by trying to make sense of something and procrastination is more about getting things right. Both behaviours interfere with hoarding issues as they become obstacles. Like all behaviours they are often linked to beliefs.

You will have noticed as you have worked through this book that you have been dealing with beliefs, feelings and behaviours. These three areas are interlinked. As discussed previously, de-cluttering alone will not help with your hoarding issues. Addressing your beliefs, feelings and behaviours will help with your problem in the longer term.

The first step in dealing with your procrastination (as with any belief, feeling or behaviour) is to recognise it. Be aware of what you are doing. The hallmark of procrastination is the self-talk that begins when something needs to be done. This internal debate gives you an indication that you are procrastinating. Another form of procrastination is discussing with a family member or friend the prospect of undertaking a task. These are subtle traps you need to be aware of.

Recognise procrastination

The first step is to recognise that you are engaging in procrastination and that it is an unhelpful behaviour. You are procrastinating because you want things to be done in a certain way, or to have a certain outcome, or to feel right. If you were to do things differently, it might mean feeling uncomfortable but in previous chapters we have discussed how you stay with or tolerate uncomfortable feelings. You will find that practising the techniques discussed earlier will help you cope better with the uncomfortable feelings and not reinforce your hoarding issues.

Once you are aware that you are procrastinating, determine the function of the procrastination. Ask yourself, What is the reason that I am having this self-talk? This will help to identify the function of the self-talk.

It is helpful to develop your formulation of the procrastination using the hoarding flower:

Once you have the function and formulation of the procrastination, ask yourself:

How helpful is this for dealing with my hoarding issues?

Is it helping in dealing with the task at hand?

What are the costs and benefits of engaging with this self-talk? Or of trying to get things just right?

These are important questions that will help you start dealing with your procrastination. However, using these questions is not enough – you also need to take the next step. Risk-taking in testing your predictions is a key component of this activity. Through testing you can find out whether or not what you think may happen, will happen. Otherwise, you fear things not turning out the way you want them to and this can stop you from actually doing them at all.

As you have worked through this book, you have actually been taking risks all along.

You have been engaging in behaviours that you would not have engaged in before – and what have you noticed so far? What has changed in the way you deal with things?

People think differently. These questions help you explore your experiences and help you make sense of them. Making the connections helps you to consolidate the experiences and reinforce the activities that you have engaged in. These connections that you have made can be added to your reclaiming flower.

Write your procrastination

Recognise that you are procrastinating and acknowledge that you are doing so. Write down what you are procrastinating about.

I am procrastinating about:

To do or not to do – procrastination

....

....

....

....

....

....

....

Develop your formulation for your procrastination.

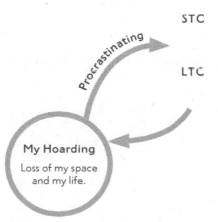

Write the advantages and disadvantages of your procrastination to help you decide on a new behaviour for dealing
with the task at hand.

The benefits or advantages of procrastinating are:

....
....
....
....
....
....
....
....
....
....
....
....
....
....
....
....
....

Short term benefits

For myself   **For others**

....

....

....

....

....

....

....

....

....

....

....

....

....

....

....

....

Long term benefits

For myself   **For others**

....

....

....

....

....

....

....

....

....

....

....

....

....

....

....

....

Short term costs

For myself   **For others**

....

....

....

....

....

....

....

....

....

....

....

....

....

....

....

....

Long term costs

For myself   **For others**

....
....
....
....
....
....
....
....
....
....
....
....
....
....
....
....

To do or not to do – procrastination

Having reviewed the advantages and disadvantages of what I am procrastinating about, my new behaviour for this task is:

....

....

....

....

....

....

....

....

You have been engaging in behaviour that you would not have engaged in before – and what have you noticed so far?

What I have noticed, by doing things differently from the normal way I do them, is:

....

....

....

....

....

247

....
....
....
....
....
....
....
....
....
....
....

I deal with things differently by:

....
....
....
....
....
....
....

....

....

....

....

....

....

....

....

....

By doing things differently you are taking risks. Test out your prediction.

To help identify your prediction, ask yourself, If I am going to do this task differently, for example, by not engaging in my procrastination, what do I think is going to happen?

....

....

....

....

....

....

....

....

....

....

....

....

....

....

....

....

Take the risk of doing things differently, not engaging in procrastination but just getting on with doing what you were intending to do.

What I found by taking risks and just getting on with the task at hand:

....

....

....

....

....

....

....

....

....

....

....

....

....

....

....

By taking risks and doing things differently from the way you normally do them, you are testing out your predictions. By testing out my prediction, I have learned that:

....

....

....

....

....

....

....

....

....

....

....

....

....

....

....

....

....

....

....

....

....

....

....

....

Ask yourself, When dealing with my hoarding issues, how helpful is it for me to have the standards, expectations and conditions that I impose when I am undertaking a task?

....

....

....

....

....

....

....

....

....

....

....

....

....

....

....

....

....

What would be more helpful for me in relation to my standards, expectations and conditions?

....

....

....

....

....

....

....

....

....

....

....

....

....

....

....

....

....

....

Another technique to help you deal with your procrastination is using mindfulness by staying with the thought, urge or feeling of wanting to do things in just the right way.

Try not to comment or engage in self-talk about the way you are feeling. Begin by just staying with the thoughts and feelings for two minutes and gradually increase the length of time. What do you notice when you stay with the thought of wanting things to be just right?

I notice:

....

....

....

....

....

....

....

....

....

As I increase the length of time that I am not engaging, I notice:

....

....

....

....

....

....

....

....

....

....

....

By not procrastinating and by carrying out the task at hand, I have noticed:

....

....

....

....

....

....

....

....

To do or not to do – procrastination

What was helpful in stopping me procrastinating was:

....

....

....

....

....

....

....

....

What was unhelpful in stopping me procrastinating was:

....

....

....

....

....

....

....

....

Accept that procrastinating is a normal behaviour and is unhelpful for you when de-cluttering and dealing with your hoarding issues.

Another technique to help you deal with your procrastination is the mindfulness technique discussed in the previous chapter. This helps you to be in the moment, when you are not comparing or judging how things were or how they are going to be. Being in the moment will help you accept the feeling as it is and by not engaging with it, you will develop your tolerance of uncomfortable feelings.

Bring to mind your thoughts, be attentive to them and let them be there; there is no need to judge or comment on them. Be aware of what is around you and aware of how it is, without judging or engaging with it.

Another mindfulness technique that is quick and easy to use is the mindfulness of sight exercise. This exercise is about seeing. Often we look at something specific, such as what is ahead of us. Truly seeing means that we open our eyes to everything around us.

Here is a simple mindfulness of sight exercise. It is short and easy to follow. Read it a few times and become familiar with it so that you can easily practise it without having to refer to it. Just carry out this exercise for short periods of time. For example, you might want to start at five minutes and gradually increase the length.

Start your mindfulness exercise by focusing on your breath.

There is no need to breathe deeply, just use your normal breathing in and out.

Have a non-judgemental awareness of the breath coming in and out.

Be aware of the place in which you find yourself. If sitting, note the position and the contact of the chair or floor on your body. If outdoors, be aware of your surroundings. Again, remember this awareness is non-judgemental.

Be aware of your environment, observe what you see, although there is no need to label the sights or describe what they are.

If you notice that your mind is engaging with your thoughts, bring your attention back to your breath, and the moment of going in and going out.

Be gentle with yourself and accept that your mind has started to engage and that is OK.

Bring your awareness back to your environment and to the sights around you.

Develop your own mindfulness techniques – whatever works for you. Mindfulness can be practised anywhere or while doing any activity. Engaging with the task at hand can be carried out mindfully. Be in the moment and carry out the task without engaging with the thoughts or uncomfortable feelings that you may be experiencing.

Family and friends

Understand what procrastination is and how it affects your friend or family member. Your knowledge can help you support them. It may be that you also benefit from reading this chapter as many of us procrastinate, particularly when we are concerned about or doubt our abilities to reach a self-imposed standard. Identifying our own unhelpful self-talk may also improve our own wellbeing, enabling us to better cope with the difficulties we encounter in supporting and in living with, or being affected by, the hoarding behaviours of our family member or friend. You may be able to help practically with the cost/benefit exercise for procrastination. Again, planning rewards for completing tasks can also help reinforce the benefits of overcoming procrastination and instead just doing it! We have previously seen that mindfulness techniques help to keep us in the moment and, although a personal experience for some, it may be motivating to practise the techniques together.

Tips

- Be aware of your procrastinating behaviour and identify what is driving it.
- Do not engage with your procrastination – get on with the task at hand.
- Recognise the triggers for your procrastinating and identify your expectations.
- Develop an attitude of acceptance that things can never be as perfect as we want them to be. Nothing is perfect.
- Practise mindfulness regularly to help with being in the moment and undertaking your tasks.

- Procrastination is common behaviour, so be accepting when you engage in it.
- Develop an attitude of acceptance that things cannot always be the way we want them.
- Develop an attitude of flexibility and apply this to everything that you undertake.
- Consider taking calculated risks every day.
- Be consistent in your approach to dealing with your procrastination.

Obstacles

'My procrastination behaviour is automatic.'

As you engage in behaviour for a long time, it becomes automatic. The first step in dealing with your procrastination is being aware of it and accepting that you are engaging with it. Write down your behaviour to make it concrete and to help you to start addressing it.

'I find that my procrastination is helpful in making sure that things are done properly.'

You may feel that procrastinating is helpful as you may predict that, without it, you might not get things right or the way you would like them to be. Start to take risks to test out your predictions. Testing your predictions is a helpful way to notice that the way you imagine things will turn out is not necessarily inevitable. Taking risks is also useful in helping you develop a more flexible way of thinking and doing things. Taking risks will help you develop new, healthier behaviours that will assist you in dealing with your hoarding issues.

'It is going to take a lot of time.'

Yes, it may take time, but the important thing is being aware of the behaviour and that you are able to do something about it. The more you practise and work on it, the easier it will become. Additionally, you will find over time and by being consistent in your approach towards the procrastination, that it will become automatic and will require less effort to deal with this behaviour.

Key messages

- Procrastination is an unhelpful behaviour that interferes with the tasks that you need to undertake when de-cluttering and dealing with your hoarding issues.
- Identify the driving factors behind the procrastination; your standards, expectations and the need for things to feel right. Recognise that standards and expectations are not helpful for your hoarding issues as they maintain the problem.
- Develop an attitude of being flexible and show willingness to try things out.
- Take risks to test out your predictions. By testing out your predictions you are in turn dealing with your standards and expectations or beliefs.
- Make mindfulness a routine in your daily activities as you can apply it to all areas that you find difficult.
- Focus on your vision from chapter two to help motivate you.

18

Back to the beginning
– review

The previous chapters have discussed interventions to help with de-cluttering and dealing with your issues. It is important to remember that you carried out this work yourself and at your own pace. It has not been an easy journey and has involved lots of hurdles and discomfort but you have made it so far. Often, we forget to review how far we have come or what we have achieved. Reviewing your progress regularly will help you recognise what has been achieved and also motivate you further to keep working on your hoarding issues.

Revisiting where you came from and where you are now can be helpful for dealing with some of the hurdles or obstacles that you will continue to face. It will also guide you to identify other areas that need attention and assist you in formulating the hoarding flower and reclaiming flower for these issues.

As discussed in part one of this book, keeping notes about what interventions have been helpful is a good practice as it will provide you with a handy toolkit that you can employ to deal with your problems. These tools can be applied to other difficulties you may be facing apart from clutter or hoarding issues. From your own experience, you will find that over the years you have had to cope with many different situations. In dealing with these, you have gained experience and you have been applying skills that you have learned over the years in many areas of your life.

Reviewing is a common practice that we all engage with on a daily basis. For example, you may feel tired and will consider why you feel that way. That is a form of review. It is done automatically – you do not even have to think about it. In terms of dealing with your clutter and hoarding, it is useful to make the review a conscious activity and part of a weekly routine.

There are many ways to review your progress; however, it is beneficial to use the tools that we have been discussing in this book as the information will be easily accessible. You will also maintain consistency as you will be reviewing from the same baseline and will be able to monitor the changes. Sometimes you may find it hard to be objective and you could consider asking a member of your family or a friend to help you.

When you are immersed in an environment, it is sometimes difficult to notice what has changed. Additionally, if you have high standards and expectations you are likely to filter out and disqualify what you have achieved to date. High standards and expectations (as we discussed in the last chapter) can be an obstacle and demotivating, as you never feel that you have done enough or achieved what you have set out to do. You will notice how important it is to be aware of your beliefs, feelings and behaviours as they play a big role in the maintenance of your difficulties.

Hoarding flower review

Reviewing your hoarding flower is a good starting point for this self-review. As you have been working on your clutter and hoarding issues, revisit the formulation you originally made in chapters 5–7. Evaluate each of the petals and write down what has changed. Highlight any areas of difficulty. The formulation can be considered to be your map and will help you to consider other interventions that you may need to take to help you deal with your problems. You can think of it as taking a different route because the current one is congested.

In part one of the book, we discussed taking photographs of your environment (see p. 37). The photographs provide visual evidence of how things are at a given moment. As you have been working through this book you have hopefully been taking photographs at various stages. Use these photographs as the means to assess what has changed. You can also use these photographs to help you rate, in terms of percentage, the progress that has been made.

In addition, revisiting the H.O.A.R.D. tool in chapter three is another way to check on the progress you have made to date and to improve your motivation. As discussed, reviewing recent photographs in a neutral environment rather than the home environment is helpful. You can also use H.O.A.R.D. to help you plan the next steps in achieving what you would like the environment to be like.

Your vision (chapter two) is another tool that you have used throughout this book – using imagery to help with your motivation. The vision is the image of how you would like the environment and your life to be. You can compare your vision with the present state of your environment and rate how close you are towards reaching your vision.

The grid technique (chapter ten) is another tool we discussed to help you feel less overwhelmed, keeping focused on one area and ensuring that the space is cleared. Keep a record of your grid and revisit the areas that are now clear. Compare it to the grid from when you first started.

The clutter image rating scale (chapter eleven) is a visual assessment tool. It was first used by professionals to rate the degree of clutter in a person's home and we adapted this tool to help you have a visual representation of how you would like the environment to be after working on it. It is also intended to help you consider the steps you would need to take to reach the level you want. It is useful as it will allow you to rate the current level of clutter compared to when you first started. You can use this with the techniques relating to scheduling (chapter four) to review your progress. Monitor the time you have spent de-cluttering and dealing with your hoarding and then incorporate the clutter tool to help assess the amount of time you need to spend in your environment for future de-cluttering.

In part one, we discussed keeping a record of the number of bags that have been discarded (see p. 40). Reviewing the record will give you an idea of the volume of material removed from your environment. This is motivating – seeing the number of bags that have left your environment highlights your progress and your ability to deal with your clutter and hoarding issues.

Reviewing can also help you assess and identify the reasons for setbacks. The process of reviewing will help you identify the obstacles and difficulties you may be experiencing. It will also allow you to identify ways to overcome these challenges.

As you have been working on your clutter and challenging your hoarding issues, you have been creative, taken risks and tested out your beliefs. You have reviewed your reclaiming flower and updated it with some of your new beliefs and behaviours and you have found new ways to deal with the challenges to the de-cluttering process.

Visual review

Revisit your formulation of the hoarding flower and identify some of the obstacles that you have faced. What kept them going? How did you cope with them? Add them to your formulation as it will help you make sense and provide you with the space to consider how you will deal with these challenges in the future.

Put the photographs that you have taken at each stage into chronological order to allow you to see the changes that have taken place in your environment. Recognise the effort you have made to reach this far. Congratulate yourself, acknowledge the difficulties you had to deal with and validate your resilience in dealing with your hoarding.

Using the same photographs, revisit the H.O.A.R.D. exercise. This will help you to recognise the progress you have made and improve your motivation to progress with the next phase of your journey.

What has Happened in this picture – H.O.A.R.D.?

....

....

....

....

....

....

....

What would I like to Overcome and what are my goals – H.O.A.R.D.?

....

....

....

....

....

....

....

Can I imagine a life without All this stuff – H.O.A.R.D.?

....

....

....

....

....

....

....

....

How are my life and Relationships affected by this problem – H.O.A.R.D.?

....

....

....

....

....

....

....

....

What would I like to <u>D</u>o about it – H.O.A.R.D.?

....

....

....

....

....

....

....

....

Bring your original vision to mind and compare it to how your environment is looking now. Ask yourself: How far am I from reaching my vision?

....

....

....

....

....

....

....

....

What percentage have I achieved so far? Rate from 0–100 per cent:

....

....

....

....

....

....

....

....

What steps must I take in order to for me to fulfil my vision?

....

....

....

....

....

....

....

....

It may be helpful to use the grid method to break down the working area into smaller sections. Review the grid by creating a new one and shading only areas that are still cluttered. Compare the first and the present grid to assess the amount of your environment that is now clear from clutter. Pin it up so that it can be a visual reminder.

Use the clutter image rating scale to rate the degree of clutter in your environment. Compare it to when you first started. You will be able to see how far you have come.

A record of the number of bags or items leaving your environment will provide concrete evidence of the impact of the efforts that you have made to de-clutter. Some people keep photographic evidence of the items that they have discarded.

As discussed, the purpose of revisiting or reviewing is not only to see the changes that have taken place but also any lack of change. It allows you the opportunity to identify obstacles and challenges that you were not aware of previously and to develop an action plan for how to deal with them.

Revisit the reclaiming flower formulation to reinforce what is working and work on the areas that have been difficult with new interventions that you may have tried out in your journey.

Family and friends

Giving clear and constructive feedback and focusing on the positive can help when your friends or family members are reviewing their progress and seeking your support. You can help to rebalance any mental filtering or disqualifying of the positives and help them to recognise their progress. Equally, if there have been obstacles, help identify these and plan ways to overcome them. Ask to see photographs that show the changes, review records and use the clutter image rating scale together, as well as celebrating how the space is now used. The process can serve to objectively acknowledge progress. The person you are supporting may wish you to be involved in planning the next steps. Review your own role as a supporter and helper; are you looking after your own wellbeing to enable you to cope the best you can in the situation and to help the other person? What has worked well in terms of you supporting and aiding them? What has not worked so well? Bring your awareness and acknowledge how things are going for you. It may be that your role is changing and adjustments may need to be made as the dynamics of your relationship with your friend or family member change.

Tips

- Keep a record of the actions that you are undertaking to deal with your clutter and hoarding issues. Place it in a safe and accessible place so that you are able to access it.

- Review on a regular basis as this will enhance your motivation to see the changes that are taking place.
- Recognise your unhelpful thinking patterns as they tend to disqualify your efforts.
- Allow others to come into your environment; they will provide feedback that can be helpful.
- Remember, reviewing and revisiting your difficulties is a positive action. It allows you to recognise what you have achieved and the obstacles that you are facing.
- Review on a regular basis; at least once a week to begin with.
- Be realistic and do not diminish how far you have come.
- If you are not making progress, acknowledge and accept that and you will be able to address it. Do not try to find reasons or justify why you have not made progress.

Obstacles

'I do not have the time to go back and look at what I did when I first started.'

Revisiting the areas where you started on your journey may appear to be time consuming but in fact it is helpful. It will highlight your ability to deal with your current difficulties with hoarding. Done regularly, you will be able to highlight the interventions that are most helpful for you and you can build on them.

'I am afraid to review things in case I am not making progress.'

This fear is real as nobody likes to feel that they are not making progress. However, it is not a negative thing to identify reasons for any lack of progress. It will help you to address these difficulties. Do not put yourself down or be hard on yourself. Accept the obstacles and revisit your formulations of your hoarding and reclaiming flowers. This may be a good opportunity to ask for support and help from those you trust.

'What if I am making too much progress?'

Congratulate yourself on the progress you have made so far. Review what has been helpful for you in your journey to reclaim your space and your life. Build on what has been helpful to reinforce it. Remind yourself of your commitment to overcoming your hoarding issues. Recognise your resilience and build on your skills. You may wish to support other people with hoarding issues.

Key messages

- Regular reviews are useful for assessing and recognising the progress that you are making.
- Build them into your activity schedule and review at least once a week.
- Reviewing will help with your motivation and encourage you to do more to overcome your hoarding issues.
- Do not feel that you cannot ask for help and support from those you trust.

- Keep a record of what is helpful and build on those interventions.
- Be consistent and use your vision to motivate you.

19

Traps

So far we have discussed many interventions you could use to help with your clutter and hoarding. In implementing those interventions, you may have experienced challenges and difficulties. We have already identified ways of dealing with some of the obstacles that you could experience. This chapter will address some of the other traps that affect your efforts to de-clutter and work on your hoarding issues.

One of the main traps is feeling overwhelmed. This is a common experience that many people have, not just in relation to hoarding but in almost every area of endeavour. One of the consequences of feeling overwhelmed is that people tend to avoid situations that make them feel uncomfortable and those that are perceived to be difficult to cope with. That may mean that the clutter in the environment is not dealt with.

Another trap is internal recycling – churning your saved items into other areas of your environment. Internal recycling is where, instead of items leaving your space in order to reduce the clutter, they are just moved into another area with the net effect of no change in the overall level of clutter. This maintains your hoarding issues. One of the common causes of internal recycling is a difficulty in making decisions. It is a common complaint amongst those who hoard that they are not able to make decisions for fear of making the wrong one.

This form of recycling is different from what we do with refuse more widely, which is essentially beneficial for the community and the environment. For an individual with a hoarding issue, recycling can become an obstacle. The beliefs related to recycling tend to be rigid and for some people the demand to ensure everything is recycled is high and counterproductive. Having these beliefs can often result in items not being discarded and remaining within the space. People with hoarding issues need to be aware of their beliefs around recycling and how they can interfere with their vision of having a clutter-free environment and re-engaging in life.

Another trap that people often fall into is not recognising the degree of what has been achieved so far. This often comes about if they disqualify the work they have undertaken so far, as it has not met their expectations or standards. Expectations and demands can have both a positive and negative impact on your hoarding. It is the negative impact that is unhelpful as it tends to lead the individual to feel demotivated by not having achieved what they set out to do.

Emotional attachments to your saved items prevent you from discarding them. This results in you keeping items based on your feelings rather than having a need to use them on a regular basis. It is normal to have emotional attachments to your belongings, especially if there is some significance attached to them, such as an item of jewellery given by a close friend. However those with hoarding issues tend to have stronger emotional attachments. Some of the beliefs that people hold are:

It is special.

It has sentimental value.

It has significance for me in what it represents.

It provides a link with the past.

My memories are attached to it.

The item has some connection to me.

The perceived need, use or value of saved items can form traps. Often people save items based on imagined need or future use. This often results in large quantities of items being hoarded for long periods of time without ever being used. Often people forget that they have these items and tend to gather even more. Some of the beliefs that people hold are:

It will be handy at another time.

I will need it in the future and will not be able to find it.

Someone may need it.

Getting rid of it is a waste of money.

The item has a life to fulfil (it contributes value).

Compulsive acquisition is another trap. Often people buy items based on the belief that they are good value and could be used in the future. Excessive amounts of things are bought or collected as a result. Often these items are never used and end up being hoarded. Some of the beliefs that people hold on this are:

I need it.

I don't want to waste it.

It is good value.

It will come in handy in the future.

There is a home waiting for it.

I may not be able to get it in the future.

Another trap is the inability to tolerate uncomfortable feelings or emotions. Emotions can be uncomfortable and people will try to find ways to reduce the discomfort. Unfortunately, sometimes the ways of coping used by people to help with these feelings perpetuate their hoarding problems. In the long term, this results in a low level of tolerance of uncomfortable feelings.

Avoidance is a major trap. It comes from a perceived fear of the intensity of the difficulty you may face or a prediction of how the situation will turn out, and a belief that you will not have the ability to deal with it or the discomfort you might experience. Avoidance leads to not facing the fear and disengaging from what you are attempting to do. As result, the areas that you fear will never get addressed or sorted. This is a major problem in the case of hoarding.

Often people avoid being in their environment so that they don't have to look at it or endure the discomfort of being in it.

Escape the trap

You can use the grid technique. Dividing your space into smaller areas will reduce the feeling of being overwhelmed. Working in a smaller area makes it more manageable, with the benefit that you can see the changes taking place. Using coloured cards in this specific area can help you maintain your focus to clear this area. Take photographs at each stage as it will help you to recognise the benefits of your efforts and celebrate that achievement.

Another way to deal with the feeling of being overwhelmed is using the clutter image rating scale to assess the severity of your clutter. Then use the scale to identify within a given period of time how you would like your environment to look. Identify this by using the photograph that best represents what you wish to achieve. Develop an action plan for what you could do to reduce the clutter to reach the level you have identified. Be realistic and set yourself achievable targets within your given time frame. You can then work at your own pace and in stages with less pressure to ensure that everything is cleared on the first attempt. Developing an action plan will help you solve problems as they arise and help you to be creative in overcoming them.

Use your activity schedule to ensure that you work consistently in your chosen area to reduce the amount of clutter.

By working consistently you will reinforce your ability to deal with the mess and also realise that things are not as severe as you had initially assumed. Mark your comments on your activity schedule, writing what you have done and achieved at that point. It will act as a record of what you have achieved when you look back and review.

The fourth method is to enlist the support of family and friends to help you with the areas that you find overwhelming. Consider the type of support that you would like to receive from them. Support can be emotional or physical. Negotiate with them how they are able to support you as you deal with de-cluttering.

When you are faced with internal recycling, remember that your objective should be for the items to leave your environment. Use the 'yes', 'no' and 'maybe' principles from chapter twelve to help you make each decision. In complex cases, it may be worthwhile using the cost/benefit analysis (see p. 69) to help you make the decision to discard the items.

Being aware of your beliefs around recycling is important. It is useful to know that almost everyone else shares similar beliefs to you about recycling. However, it is the rigidity of your beliefs that has a negative impact on your hoarding issues. Learning to be flexible and taking the risk of discarding items without recycling is helpful. It is important to remember that all items that are discarded are eventually recycled even if they take a different route than the one you intended. If you are still finding it difficult to discard your saved items, it may be helpful to revisit your vision to gain the perspective of what your intentions are in relation to your hoarding.

As discussed above, keep a record of the work that you have undertaken and the number of bags or items that have been discarded. When you feel despondent or feel that you have not achieved much, refer back to your record of what has been done so that it can remind you and help you recognise just what you have achieved. Place this record where you can see it easily. It may be useful to use coloured card to keep your attention.

Emotional attachments are normal, but if you have hoarding issues the number of items saved is usually excessive. You will need to recognise the role of emotions in saving items and that it may not be helpful. It is reasonable to save items based on need or daily utility. Recognise that emotional attachment is part of the unhelpful thinking pattern and use the cost/benefit analysis to help you decide how best to deal with the items.

You will need to challenge your beliefs about the perceived need for these items. These beliefs maintain your hoarding problems. These key questions can be helpful in dealing with these beliefs:

When was the last time I used this item?

If there was a fire or a robbery and all these things were lost, would I be able to function?

How likely is it that I will need to use these items?

If I needed this item in the future, would I be able to get it from another source?

Challenging your beliefs about emotional attachments and perceived needs using supporting evidence can be helpful. Write down your beliefs and document the evidence for and against each, reviewing it to help you have a more balanced view of the situation and be able to deal with it accordingly.

Compulsive acquisition is a major problem. Not every individual who hoards has this problem but a majority do. It is helpful to acknowledge the need to acquire items and then learn to resist it. Identify the things that you compulsively acquire, such as books or clothes. You will notice that there is a pattern and there are triggers that lead to you acquiring items. For example, going into charity shops can be a trigger. You may choose not to visit charity shops on your own or choose the shops where you are less likely to engage in buying more. Limit the time you spend in places where you are more likely to acquire items. Learn to say 'No' by questioning yourself:

Do I need this item?

Will I use it immediately?

What are the reasons for me getting this item?

If I had not seen it, would I have felt that I needed it?

These questions will help you to step back so that you can get a better perspective of the situation and deal with it better.

Another technique that could be helpful is making a note of the item you liked, leaving it and continuing your shopping. Then ask yourself later whether you need it without going back to the shop or area where the item is located. You may find that your desire to have and obtain the item has lessened.

Always use your original vision as a tool to help you remain focused on what you are trying to aim for and achieve.

It is important to try to develop a higher level of tolerance to uncomfortable feelings. As discussed previously, recognising, validating and accepting the way you are feeling are good steps. Try not to engage with your uncomfortable feelings. Start by not engaging over short periods of time and gradually increase these periods. Remind yourself that these feelings will pass and the discomfort will reduce. Use the mindfulness exercises discussed over previous chapters. Enlist the support of your family and friends to help you cope with the uncomfortable feelings.

In dealing with your avoidance, it is useful to revisit your formulation of your hoarding flower and identify the role that avoidance has in maintaining your problem and how it becomes a trap you can get stuck in. Recognise when you have not avoided things, and what you gained from that. If you perceive it to be too difficult, break it down into smaller steps so that it becomes more manageable.

Writing it down

Often we try to deal with our challenges or obstacles by thinking about them. It is helpful in the first instance to write them down. Writing them down will help validate the difficulty, make it more concrete and help you focus on dealing with it. In addition, writing it down will help you identify the actual trap or obstacle.

Revisit your formulation of the hoarding flower to help you make sense of how these traps, and your ways of coping with them, impact on your hoarding issues.

My current obstacle, challenge, difficulty or trap is:

....

....

....

....

....

....

....

....

Once you have identified the obstacle, challenge, difficulty or trap, use the strategies above to help you deal with it.

Having identified what the problem is, my next steps are:

....

....

....

....

....

....

....

....

....

Review the steps that you have taken to deal with the challenge you were faced with.

Having put into action the next steps for dealing with my obstacle, challenge, difficulty or trap, I noticed:

....

....

....

....

....

....

....

....

....

Reflect on how you have dealt with the obstacle, challenge, difficulty or trap above and write down what you learned and what that says about you.

In the experience of dealing with the challenge above, I have learned:

....

....

....

....

....

....

....

....

....

I have dealt with these challenges and what this says about me is:

....

....

....

....

....

....

....

....

My strengths are:

....

....

....

....

....

....

....

....

....

Remember that all the techniques suggested in previous chapters to help you deal with the challenges you face can be applied across the other difficulties in your life.

Step back and review how you have dealt with your challenges and coped with them.

Family and friends

Depending on the level of support you have agreed will work for your family member or friend, there are many options for helping with obstacles and recognising traps. Familiarise yourself with the types of trap discussed above and, if your relationship with the person dealing with hoarding issues allows, you could raise a warning flag if you think they are falling into one. For example, you could question rigid recycling, compulsive buying, the future need for items and other unhelpful beliefs. To help overcome the traps or obstacles, gently question what needs to be done to move forward, what has worked for them before when dealing with similar difficulties, or just ask if there is anything that they would like you to do to help. Remind them of their vision and be available. Agree methods of communication such as phone, email, social media or discussion in person. This will depend on distance and preferences and will ensure your support is easy to access. Try to remember or refer to notes of what has worked before to help overcome the current difficulty.

Tips

- Accept the obstacles, difficulties or challenges that you are facing.
- Reflect on your past experiences and how you have coped with them. Draw on these experiences to help you deal with them in the present moment.

- If it is too difficult, ask for support from family and friends.
- Break it down into smaller steps which you will find easier to manage.
- Always write down your action plan.
- Keep a record of what has helped you as a resource for any potential difficulties you may face in the future.
- Acknowledge that obstacles, challenges, difficulties and traps are part and parcel of life and you face them on a daily basis.
- Recognise your ability to cope and deal with situations that are difficult. People often underestimate their ability to deal with the challenges they face.
- Try not to avoid the challenges but instead face them.

Obstacles

'I find that I avoid dealing with my hoarding issues when they get too difficult.'

Avoidance is a normal reaction when faced with difficulties. However, you will have noticed that avoidance keeps your problems going. Try to face your difficulties rather than avoid them. If it helps, break the difficulty into smaller steps and face each separately.

'I do not have the ability to deal with my difficulties.'

Remember that you face difficulties on a daily basis and cope with them. It is easy to forget your ability to face challenges. Step back and recognise your resilience when faced with these difficulties and look at how you have coped and managed so far. Each situation is an opportunity to learn and develop new and healthier coping mechanisms.

'The difficulties appear to be never-ending.'

Sometimes you are bombarded with one difficulty after another. This is because you are dealing with an aspect of your life that is difficult. The problem you have is long-standing and it will take time to overcome. Deal with one difficulty as it arises rather than getting worried about the potential challenges you may face.

Key messages

- It is normal to experience challenges when dealing with your hoarding issues.
- Revisit your formulation of the hoarding flower to have an understanding of how these challenges affect you and the ways you have tried to cope with them.
- You have the ability and skills to deal with traps as they appear. Recognise your strengths.
- Be flexible and creative to adapt your skills to deal with your challenges.
- Use your vision to keep you focused on dealing with your hoarding issues.

20

Keep going

If you have worked through the book to this point, you have hopefully made a lot of progress and are aware of a significant improvement in reclaiming your space and your life. This does not mean it is the end of your journey. In fact, this is just the beginning. Each chapter has been written with the aim of introducing you to new skills and exercises that you can continue to use as you de-clutter and deal with your hoarding issues.

You have achieved a lot so far, but the key thing is to keep up the momentum and ensure that you continue working towards your vision. In the end, we hope that you are able to function fully in your space and use it for what it was intended.

This journey does not only focus on your clutter or on your hoarding but also on your life more widely. Here are some tips.

Review the notes that you have made and use the exercises that you have found most helpful in achieving your vision. Make regular reviews of your progress and use the principles described by going back to the basics.

Revisit the tips and key messages – they are intended to provide you with a quick reminder of the main points of each chapter.

Foster a willingness to try things or test them out. Be creative and flexible, as often situations may not turn out as you would like them to. Work on your expectations and standards, which will help you in the longer term when things aren't they way you would like them to be.

Abandon avoidance. Avoidance only makes things worse. You are resilient and you have made it this far in your life. Recognise your inner strength. Show kindness, beginning with yourself. Being kind is being compassionate. Compassion allows growth, so let yourself grow.

Where possible, try to help someone else. There is no better way of learning and reinforcing your skills than by helping someone else. This will also help you develop an attitude of sharing and reflection. In order to help someone else, you will need to reflect on what you have tried and tested.

Life is full of uncertainty, so develop an attitude of curiosity like that of a cat; playful yet still engaged in what you are doing. Finding out and exploring means taking risks. Take risks, as they mean you are pushing the boundaries and you will discover that some of your fears or anxieties are unwarranted.

Keep a record of your achievement. Often, when we are feeling low or despondent we can forget what we have done. Praise yourself for your efforts and the hard work on your journey to reclaim your space and your life. Engage fully in all the activities you are trying out.

Part three

Reclaiming your life

As you are working on your hoarding issues, don't forget that life goes on. You mustn't neglect other activities – that is all part of being a person. Developing a healthy balance of work, pleasure, rest and me-time is all part of the plan for reclaiming your life. Often we get so involved in getting through life, we forget the need for making me-time. On the other hand, there can be too much me-time, where everything else (like your hoarding) gets ignored.

You will have noticed that one of the key themes in this book has been the involvement of family and friends. As people, we are social creatures. However, our hoarding issues can cause us to feel shame and to fear that others will reject or judge us due to our problems. As a result, we lose contact with those who are near and dear to us. If you have started engaging with your family and friends more as you have worked through this book, you may have found quite the opposite. Family and friends care about who we are, not about our environment. At the end of the day, it is the person that matters. You may have found, in fact, that friends and family have been supportive and want to help. This in itself can feel daunting.

At the beginning of this book, we talked about your vision of how you would like things to be. We asked you to have a vision of a reclaimed life. Each and every one of us has a vision of how we would like our life to be. We take measures to try to achieve that vision. Sometimes, there are obstacles that stop us realising that vision. You have made progress with your hoarding issues. Now it is time to address your vision of reclaiming your life. It is helpful to recall your vision and consider what it feels like, as you work through this chapter, to help you realise it.

In part two we discussed scheduling your time to better deal with your hoarding issues. If you consider your daily routine, you probably don't often think about some of the activities you engage in, such as eating and drinking, going to work or shopping. These activities are part of your life and you rarely have to consider planning undertaking them in great detail. For example, you automatically know that you will need to buy or prepare food at lunchtime. In order to bring in activities outside your normal routine you can use the scheduling we discussed in chapter four. Over a period of time, these activities can also become routine and enhance your quality of life.

What were the activities that I used to enjoy in the past?

....

....

....

....

....

....

....

....

What are the activities that I enjoy now?

....

....

....

....

....

....

....

....

Often we feel that we are unable to identify the activities that we would like to engage in, or we feel that we do not have the money. But there are many activities you can undertake that do not involve having to pay. The key thing is that you are motivated and willing to undertake them. A good resource to locate these activities is your local library. The local council often organises activities for the community. Libraries are the information point for your local community. It is a good place to start to locate activities that might interest you and provide you with the opportunity to be engaged and to socialise.

What can I do to start engaging in some of the activities that I enjoy?

....

....

....

....

....

....

....

Who would I like to do these activities with?

....

....

....

....

....

....

....

Community events provide an opportunity to meet other people and help develop a network of friends and activities for yourself. This will help you to feel part of your community and develop a support network. Support can take many different forms. Having contact with other people helps us to connect with what is going outside our own lives and helps normalise our difficulties.

Write your chosen activities down in your activity schedule and, where possible, highlight them with a different colour. This will serve as a reminder of what you are intending to do. Take the risk of engaging in activities that you have never done before. There is no way you will know whether you will enjoy something or not without trying it out, just as there is no way to tell if certain foods are tasty or not without trying them first. Reflect back on your life and the activities in which you have taken part and consider how many of those were unfamiliar before you tried them.

Voluntary work can be a good way to build structured activities into your life and to meet new people. The benefit of volunteering is that you can do as much or as little as you want. It will allow you the flexibility to engage in other activities. Volunteering is also about giving something back to the community. Channelling your energy into helping others is rewarding and fulfilling.

Most local newspapers – these can be found in your local library – will advertise activities in your local area. Search the internet for activities in other areas, then contact friends and family members and check whether they are aware of activities that sound interesting.

Consider taking a course. We are constantly engaging in some form of learning, both formally and informally. Not all courses have an academic requirement and some just need your participation. Remember, you bring your own knowledge, skills and life experiences that you can share with others. Courses are about sharing and learning from each other.

Another option you may wish to consider is attending lectures. At these lectures there is an opportunity to meet others who share the same interests as you. This is a good way to be part of a group of people who share similar ideas. It is possible that these lectures could lead to associated activities.

All these activities are a good way to meet other people and develop a network of friends. Having this network will help you structure your time with a balance of social activities. In addition, being with other people will provide you with social support.

Part of reclaiming your life is also beginning to allow others into it. There may come a time when you would like others to visit you. This can be an incentive to help you keep working on your hoarding and ensure that your space is maintained in the way you would like it to be in your vision. Inviting others into your life also gives you a stronger connection with the world outside your home.

Attend a support group, which is a good opportunity to meet others who may have similar difficulties. It is often easier to engage with others you feel may be able to relate to you and not judge you. The support group can also be a place for you to share your experiences of dealing with your hoarding issues that may be helpful to others.

If you meet another person who needs support, be a buddy for them as it will also be a way to reinforce what you have learned and to practise your skills. Remember, you don't have to support others exclusively with their hoarding, as just being a friend can be of great benefit.

There may always be a lurking fear of stigma and prejudice. Challenge your fears by starting to disclose your hoarding issues with family, friends and those you trust. You will be surprised to find that people are generally supportive and non-judgemental. You may get offers of help and it can be a good opportunity to allow others into your home. Remember, you have control about how much you wish to disclose and the degree of access you grant others. You can make an opportunity to do things with others outside your home by, for example, going out shopping or having coffee.

Live in your home, ensuring that all the spaces are being used for what they were designed for. The kitchen should be used for cooking your meals, and the bedroom for sleeping in. Remember, the lifestyle you developed around the clutter and hoarding has only maintained the problem. Changing your habits and using spaces in which you once hoarded items are part of reclaiming your life.

Decorate your space the way you want it to be. One of the consequences of clutter is that you are not able to see the colour of your walls, floor or carpets. The lack of colour can have a negative impact on your mood and weaken your motivation to engage in activities. Colour brightens up the environment, improves the way you feel and allows you to appreciate your room. Spend time in the space to have ownership of it, acknowledge what you have achieved and the effort that you have put into it to get there.

Gradually, over time, you are not only reclaiming your space, but also engaging with activities to reclaim your life. The more you start interacting with others, the more likely it is that this will lead to your participating in activities involving others outside your home.

Family and friends

Depending on the level of difficulties your friend or family member is dealing with and the level of your involvement, it may be important for you also to reclaim your life. Sometimes we become so involved in supporting another that we have little time for ourselves outside of our routine activities such as work, household tasks and family responsibilities. Reading this chapter may have been equally helpful for you. Perhaps you can plan some activities with your friend or family member that would give you both pleasure and a structure for the day? You could organise a social activity, accompany them to a café or help to find activities that meet their interests. It could be creative, involve music or art, history or current affairs or it could be fitness linked or fun. Encouragement in many cases will be motivating and will help. Timing is important, however, so remember that this is their decision and choice. Including the person close to you in some relevant activity or family, community or social event may help them to move towards their vision and to reclaim their life. Talk about their vision and the steps that are needed to enable this. Ensure that the steps are appropriate. It is fine to encourage them out of a comfort zone into a stretch zone, but it may not be helpful for someone to leap too far and be overwhelmed or put into a situation that is not yet enjoyable. Some people may need to push the boundaries of their comfort zone until confidence builds by taking small steps. Helping to decorate or put colour into the newly cleared space and inviting others could support the person close to you in reclaiming their life. If you are working towards and doing activities that are in line with the valued directions you say are important for you in your life, then this is likely to increase feelings of wellbeing. A valued direction may relate to family, relationships, social life, work, spirituality, health and fitness, creativity, hobbies, community service or many other areas. The vision created by your friend or family member is likely to encompass what is most important to them.

Tips

- Engage with your family and friends.
- Make a note of the activities that you find interesting. Find out more about these activities.
- Take the risk of trying things out.
- Try living out of your comfort zone; do things that you do not normally do.

- Recognise the journey you have taken so far to reach this point in your life.
- Living your life is about being yourself and honouring yourself as an individual.
- It is healthy to engage with activities outside your home.
- When you are out and about, make a note of anything you find interesting. Explore whatever that may be and find out more about it.
- Show an air of curiosity, find out more when you interact with others and while engaging in activities.

Obstacles

'I do not have any friends.'

It is not important that you have friends to engage in activities. However, an attitude of being willing to engage with others will help. By engaging with others you will gradually make friends and start doing things together. Remember, strangers are just friends you have not met.

'It has been many years since I have done anything outside my home. I do not have any ideas where to go.'

Sometimes it can feel daunting to consider doing things that you have not done for a long time. A helpful way is sometimes just going out and spending time outside your home. Visit the local library and get used to an environment where there are people about but you do not have to interact. It can also be useful to look at local activities that are advertised there to identify any that may interest you.

Try to talk to others there who may be able to give you some ideas.

'I cannot allow anyone into my home; they will be disgusted and think that I am mentally ill.'

This is a normal and understandable fear or concern, that you will be judged by others and thought of in a negative way, which provokes anxiety. If you have had the experience of involving your family and friends, you will have noticed that they accept you as a person rather than judge you as being the problem. Others may have anxieties about how to approach you as they do not wish to cause you distress. However, you are an individual who has a problem rather than a problem person. You will find that, as you allow others into your life and your home, they will be generally accepting and supportive. It is useful to discuss your fears with those you are with as this will air your concerns and reduce the fears of your family and friends.

Key messages

- Reclaiming your life is part of dealing with your hoarding issues.
- Use your vision of a reclaimed life to motivate you.
- Your interactions with your friends and family arc a part of the process of reclaiming your life.
- Engagement with activities outside your home environment is good way to enrich your life with new activities and opportunities to meet new people.
- Take risks by doing things that are outside of your

comfort zone, meet new people and be willing to try new, exciting things.

- Recognise your strengths and resilience in having coped with life so far. Use those strengths to take the next step.
- Build on the activities you enjoy and put them into your schedule so they can be carried out regularly.
- When you are ready, invite others into your home. This will change your relationship with your environment, making it a social place rather than a place that is associated with your hoarding.

Part four

Maintain your gains and prevent relapses

You may remember that in part one we discussed writing down exercises that work for you. The reason is to help you continue in your journey to reclaim your space and your life. Having started the work and made progress to reach your vision does not mean that the efforts end here. In keeping going there needs to be ongoing work. This may not be as intense, but nevertheless effort needs to be made.

One of the most important things to remember is to review the photographs of your space before, during and after your de-cluttering. Reflect on the progress you have made and the energy and effort that has got you there. Remind yourself:

What did I have to do to get here – what steps did I take?

....

....

....

....

....

....

....

....

....

Now ask yourself, What do I need to do to keep this place as it is?

....

....

....

....

....

....

....

....

Maintain your gains and prevent relapses

What are the reminders to get me started?

....

....

....

....

....

....

....

....

What keeps me going?

....

....

....

....

....

....

....

....

Who is there to support me?

....
....
....
....
....
....
....
....

What support do I need?

....
....
....
....
....
....
....
....
....

How do I negotiate this with them?

....

....

....

....

....

....

....

....

Write all of these down as they will serve you well.

It is important to remember how you have structured your new life with the helpful routines. One of the key messages in the basics chapter in part two was to make time, meaning that you should maintain an activity schedule that you can follow daily. It is like being on a diet and changing your eating habits to include healthier choices. Life is full of demands and there are certain things that we have to do, such as breathe, eat and sleep. These are things that we do automatically and some activities fall into the same category.

The key theme throughout this book has been reclaiming your space and your life. The way to get better at doing anything is by doing it consistently; for example, if you want to cook well, you will need to cook often and take risks while cooking. Likewise, in maintaining the gains you have made and continuing to work on your hoarding issues, you need to challenge yourself and take risks in facing the things that you have saved, making decisions and de-cluttering.

Revisit your vision regularly and recognise your journey from where you started to where you have got to now. Recognise your efforts – it has not been easy but it has been worth it. Look at photographs from when you started and now. Identify the changes and recognise what they mean to you. Capture the feeling when looking at these photographs and identify ways to keep this feeling going. Share your progress with others such as your friends and family. Let them celebrate what you have achieved so far. Make them a part of your journey. They do not have to be doing things for you but can just be there and share the changes with you. It will make a big difference.

Beware of the trap of taking it easy. It is human nature to want to cruise, but you will still need to do some work – just not as much as before. You are now in the maintenance phase that involves less time but requires being consistent and keeping to a routine. Recognise the obstacles you have faced on your journey to reclaim your space and your life. Remind yourself of the steps that you have taken to overcome these obstacles.

Accountability is important in the progress you make. Ultimately you are accountable only to yourself. For some, it is helpful to be able to share with someone else how you are doing and how you have got on. Make a note of the activities that you have undertaken and highlight those that have been helpful. It may be useful to revisit and repeat them – you may find that the more you engage in these activities, the better you get at them.

Developing your hoarding flower helped you make sense of how your beliefs, emotions and behaviours play a role in keeping your hoarding going. It is useful to review the flower regularly. Formulations are dynamic and change as we alter our behaviour, attitude and the way we deal with our emotions. Your formulation is a map of your difficulties, but it also provides you with the keys or solutions. Build on your reclaiming flower as this will help reinforce the gains that you have made to date, bolster your motivation and reframe the beliefs you hold about the things you used to save.

Having a daily routine, such as dedicating a specific period of time to sorting and clearing your space, is helpful. Consider this period as equivalent to your other daily routines, such as going to work, eating and other activities which over time have become ingrained and automatic and you will be able to undertake it without having to think about it.

Break down your plan for dealing with your hoarding issues into smaller tasks as this will be less overwhelming and will enable you to work on manageable areas with the grid method. You will see improvement easily and this will increase your motivation. Recognise the areas that you have managed to de-clutter. Highlight them using coloured card so that it draws your attention to what you have achieved so far. Spend time feeling and relishing the space you have regained.

Tone down the demand you feel to be perfect and address the beliefs that maintain that demand. Recognise the beliefs that interfere with your progress and the new ones that you have developed to help deal with your hoarding. Always engage in behaviour that reinforces the new, helpful beliefs. Use the 'yes', 'no' and 'maybe' piles and recognise your self-talk. This method reduces the time you spend checking and making decisions.

Notice unhelpful thinking patterns to recognise the way you interpret a situation and the impact it has on you. Beliefs and assumptions serve a purpose but need to be flexible to help you function better.

You will have encountered obstacles along this journey; reflect on them and how you overcame them. Ask yourself, What does the way I deal with specific obstacles say about my ability to deal with the challenges I face?

....

....

....

....

....

....

....

....

This will help you recognise your resilience or your inner strength to face the obstacles you have encountered. As people, we face challenges on a daily basis and just deal with them and go about our business without being aware of that fact.

Be aware of the traps that you get into, such as rumination and procrastination. Catch them early so that they do not spiral out of control and take over your intention to reclaim your space and your life.

Take risks. There are no guarantees in life and taking risks helps us learn and adapt to situations better. Without taking risks we never know. Reflect back on the risks you have taken so far.

What has the outcome been in relation to your hoarding issues?

Has the behaviour of taking risks helped you become stronger?

In your experience, what are the benefits of having taken risks?

What have you learned when you have taken risks?

Be kind to yourself. Learn to show yourself kindness and understanding. We are able to be kind and understanding towards others. One act of kindness is being patient in your journey. Your hoarding issues have been there for a long time and have taken many years to develop to the point that they have become difficult. Accept that changes are going to take time and that you are working on it gradually, not just in de-cluttering but in dealing with what keeps the hoarding going.

It is human nature to want change to happen quickly. Progress is slow, but recognise where you have come from and where you are going. Review your hoarding flower and reclaiming flower regularly and make changes and updates. Reinforce your new beliefs by carrying out activities that are consistent with those beliefs. For example, your belief may now be, If I do not read every single paper, it does not mean I will be less knowledgeable. The new behaviour to reinforce this may be: not reading every single paper, or recycling the paper even if you have not read it. By changing your behaviour, you will help reinforce your new way of thinking and reduce the significance of the old beliefs.

There will be days when you feel that you have not done enough. Accept that this is normal and do not be hard on yourself. Doing this will only demotivate you and lead to you not wanting to face or work on your clutter and hoarding issues. This book has adopted an approach of teaching you to be flexible. Being flexible will help you make more progress as you adapt to changes that are taking place. Review what you have done so far to see the progress you have made.

It is often helpful to create a collage of your journey to reclaim your space and your life. The photographs that you have taken can help create the collage. It is a good way to review the progress and changes you have made as you have visuals. The collage tells your story and what you have done to reach this point.

Remember to live fully in the space you have reclaimed. Living and enjoying your space is a good way to help you recognise what you have gained and will provide you with the motivation to keep working on your hoarding. Engage with others and invite them into your environment; this will ensure that you keep the focus on freeing your space from clutter. This is also a way to celebrate what you have achieved and help you strive to continue working on maintaining it and dealing with your ongoing hoarding issues. Additionally, others will be able to provide you with support.

There may be occasions where you feel that you have relapsed. For example, you may acquire newspapers and not discard them. Call this a setback rather than a relapse. Review the hoarding flower and reclaiming flower to help you get back on track and formulate a plan of action.

Be consistent in your approach to dealing with your clutter and hoarding issues. The consistency will help in maintaining a routine and structure for your progress.

My relapse prevention plan

Having read the notes above and the notes you have made as you have worked through this book, spend some time developing a strategy.

What are my ongoing problems?

Write down your current issues in relation to your hoarding and their impact on you. The consequences are important as they will help you focus on the need to work on current issues.

What keeps my problems going?

Make a note of factors that keep your problems going: for example, your beliefs, feelings and behaviour. Refer back to your formulation of the hoarding flower.

What did I learn from undertaking the exercises in this book?

Write down your experience of undertaking the exercises – what was helpful to you? Did you ask family and friends to help, for instance? What you write will form your top tips for change. Write what you would say to a friend who had hoarding issues and was asking for help.

What do I need to do to continue working on my hoarding issues?

Write your plan for continuing to work on your hoarding issues. Sometimes it may be useful to imagine that you are helping a friend who has hoarding issues – write the steps they would need to take to deal with the problem.

What are the potential obstacles and how will I overcome them?

Make a list of all the challenges and obstacles that you have faced in dealing with your hoarding issues. Write how you dealt with each one, including the steps you took and what helped. Refer to the list above. This will also help you solve future challenges that you may face.

Family and friends

Supporting the person who is overcoming their hoarding issues in the maintenance phase is less intense but is still vital. It is easy to think that the job is done, but keeping the living spaces clear is a daily task. Continue to be there for them and give the support that has worked for them. This is likely to have its own rewards. You may wish to ask how you can be involved in their relapse prevention plan and what would be most valued. It may be that you can continue by taking photographs, recording, taking items to the charity shop or whatever was helpful previously. Respect their routine and help clear, or help when difficulties and obstacles arise, as you did before. The emphasis may shift to being involved in pleasurable activities in their reclaimed space and life. It could be that new support, such as decorating or organising work in their home, may be most welcomed. Enjoy the space, the results and the reclaimed life!

Tips

- Be consistent in your approach to dealing with your hoarding issues. Each intervention you implement involves working at many levels – on beliefs, emotions and behaviour.
- On a daily basis, write down what has been helpful and what you will use regularly.

- Review your progress regularly using the photographs you take of the areas on which you are working to monitor the changes that are taking place.
- Look at the photographs of the area you are working on to see the changes that are taking place. Sometimes it is hard to notice change. Photographs can help you step back in seeing.
- Be creative in your approach. Be flexible as plans change.
- Be willing to target another area that is easier and come back to the difficult one later.
- Engage family and friends to help when you need additional support.
- Maintain a structure and routine that incorporates working on your hoarding on a daily basis.
- Recognise the progress you are making and share with family and friends as it helps to reinforce the progress. Getting positive feedback is helpful.
- Revisit the H.O.A.R.D tool regularly to keep your motivation going.
- Review your relapse prevention plan on a daily basis as it will help you focus on the key areas that you still need to work on.

Obstacles

'I do not know where to begin.'

It is helpful to review this book from the beginning and look at your notes. The notes will help you identify what has been useful and you can incorporate that into your relapse prevention plan.

'It is hard to keep a daily routine; I tend to do it when I can.'

It is important to have a daily routine. Like other activities in your life, it will help you to have a structure. A daily routine means that you are dealing with your hoarding issues on a daily basis and with the aim of reducing the clutter.

'How is the relapse prevention plan going to help me? I already have the book.'

It is good that you have a book that is comprehensive. But the relapse prevention plan is a summary of your current hoarding issues and it has the key interventions that have been helpful for you. Crucially, it highlights what *you* have put into place to deal with *your* hoarding. It is also a quick reminder and is helpful if you are dealing with a difficulty – the plan will provide you with a quick guide to dealing with it. Developing the plan can also help you review where you are in terms of your hoarding, what areas you need to work on and how to set up a plan to deal with those areas.

Key messages

- Develop your relapse prevention plan as it will help consolidate your experience of dealing with your clutter and hoarding.
- Take regular photographs of the area that you are working in to help you evaluate your progress.
- Revisit your formulation of the hoarding and

reclaiming flowers regularly. The formulation will provide you with the solutions to deal with your problems, recognise the gains you have made and build on your motivation to overcome your problem

- Use H.O.A.R.D. to help you recognise changes and motivate you to work on additional areas.
- Put into practice the interventions in your relapse prevention plan which you have recognised as being helpful in order to become better at them.
- Keep the relapse prevention plan in a place where you can access it easily.
- Share your relapse prevention plan with your family and friends as they may be able to help you deal with the obstacles you face.
- Recognise your gains, record them and celebrate what you have achieved.

Remember, this is a self-help book. It will not solve all your problems but it can provide you with some elements that you may find helpful. As you progress through your journey, you will also discover and try other bits and pieces along the way that will aid you.

We would like to praise you for your courage in dealing with a complex problem, your strength in taking each step, and your wisdom in making the decisions. We wish you success in each and every step of your personal journey to reclaim your space and your life. Never forget where you came from and where you are heading. Keep your vision alive and burning bright until you realise it.

Appendix

Tips

Here is a summary of the golden rules for dealing with your hoarding:

- Use your vision to motivate you.

- Take photographs or make drawings at the beginning and at regular intervals to monitor your progress.

- Develop personalised formulations using the hoarding flower and reclaiming flower.
  - ★ Refer to your own hoarding flower formulation as it will help you understand the way your beliefs, emotions and behaviour maintain your problem.

- Refer to your personalised reclaiming flower formulation as your guide to reclaiming your space and your life.

- Review both your formulations regularly and note changes with the progress you are making in dealing with the clutter and hoarding issues.
  - ★ Use your activity schedule to help you to work consistently on a daily basis.

- ★ Work consistently in one grid area before moving to another. This will help you better notice the reduction in clutter, which will instil hope and the possibility of change.

- Use the coloured card system to help you keep focused on the area you are working on.
    - ★ Move items that are being de-cluttered out of your environment rather than to another room. This is called internal recycling or churning and maintains hoarding issues.

- Each time you leave the house, take a bag out to discard or give away. This will help you develop new patterns of dealing with your clutter. It will also help develop the habit of removing unwanted items from your space.
    - ★ Contact a friend or family member that you trust and inform them of your intention for the day, for example de-cluttering the space. Call them later to let them know of your progress. If you are not able to contact anyone, write down your intention and, at the end of the day, review and update it.

- Keep a written record of what you have achieved each day, such as the number of bags discarded and the area worked on, etc.

- Identify the broad category of items in each area and have clear criteria for the 'yes' and 'no' piles for each of those categories.

- Look at each item quickly and make an instant decision about its destination pile.

- Use yes, no and maybe principles.

- Avoid rechecking, as rechecking will create doubts.
  * Use self-talk constructively in dealing with the underlying mechanisms that maintain your hoarding problem.

- Practise recognising your unhealthy thinking patterns (they are normal) on a daily basis.

- Acknowledge your feelings. Feelings are normal. Identify your coping behaviours and question yourself about their role and their perceived helpfulness in overcoming your hoarding issues.

- Learn to tolerate uncomfortable feelings.

- Develop an attitude of flexibility and creativity. Flexibility and creativity will give you the freedom to deal with your hoarding with less resistance.
  * Behave and act in accordance with your new helpful beliefs.

- Recognise your standards and expectations as they are an obstacle to you and lead to procrastination.

- Develop your tolerance to rumination and procrastination by staying with those thoughts but not engaging with them.

- Practice mindfulness on a daily basis. You can do it

in practically any activity by being in the moment and adopting an attitude of not evaluating or judging. Experience the experience as it is.

* Be creative in dealing with de-cluttering and your hoarding issues. Sometimes, despite our best efforts, plans do not work out. Being creative will allow you to focus in a different way.

• Be aware of the traps and make a point of reminding yourself of them. You will recognise them earlier and not let them become an obstacle.

* Engage in activities outside your home; reclaim what you enjoy and wish to fulfil.
* Take risks each day. Be curious when taking risks as it is an opportunity for discovery.
* Test out your predictions and do not let unproven predictions stop you from achieving your vision.
* Be kind to yourself – develop compassion in understanding your problem. Recognise your resilience in making it this far.

• Seek professional help if you have other issues.

Unhelpful thinking patterns
Black-and-white thinking

This involves viewing things in a concrete way. In this way there are no grey or in-between areas. Things are either good or bad. Black-and-white thinking is inflexible and rigid and leads us to seeing a global view in the same way.

This thinking does not allow any room to consider other perspectives. Let's look at the example of a rainy day. We could say that the day is wet and it is bad (black and white) or we could consider that it is wet, the temperature is mild and the garden is getting watered, leaving the situation not as negative as we originally considered it.

Labelling

The labelling of yourself, others or a situation in a negative way. For example, I am useless, they are bad, the place is a tip. Labelling is not helpful because when we apply labels we tend to behave in a manner that supports our badge. For example, you might view your own environment as being beyond help. You may have labelled it as such and therefore it is highly unlikely that you are going to try and sort the place out.

Mental filtering

Mental filtering happens when you disregard the positive around you. An example would be if you had worked hard on de-cluttering your environment but then you choose to ignore all the work and focus instead on the areas that you have not worked on. Another example could be remembering all the things that have not gone as well as planned during the day. Mental filtering affects you – it is demotivating and effectively blanks out all the good work.

Disqualifying the positive

Disqualifying the positive means not recognising the good or positive aspects of the situation. For example: you have cleared out a section of your room but when asked about what you have done in your environment, you say, 'I have not done much.' Consider the impact of not recognising what you have done; you are likely to feel disheartened and less motivated.

Mind reading

We believe we know what other people are thinking about us or how they will react to us. For example, if you are considering telling your close friends or family about your hoarding problem, you might have thoughts that they are going to react in a negative way and, as a result, you do not tell them and do not receive the support that could be offered. In reality, it is often the case that others do not react in the way that we think they are going to.

Emotional reasoning

When we use our feelings as evidence of a situation, we are emotionally reasoning. In preparing to de-clutter your space you might say, 'I do not feel that I can do it' and, as a result, you do not even try. You'll never know whether you are able or unable to clear your space without trying it out first. We often use emotional reasoning and it prevents us from finding out the reality of the situation.

Catastrophising

We leap straight to thinking about a catastrophe when we picture the worst-case scenario. For example, imagine you allow a friend or family member to help and you jump to the conclusion that they will disrupt everything and throw away your belongings without your knowledge. Another example of this is when you decide to throw away some old newspapers and you worry that you might need them in the future. This leads you to feel anxious. Jumping to conclusions tends to affect you by making you feel anxious and worry excessively.

Demands

You have high standards and expectations for yourself or others. These demands affect you as they are rigid and hard to meet. For example, when de-cluttering your space, if you have an expectation that you will clear a certain amount and then fail to reach that expectation, it can lead you to feel demotivated and experience negative emotions. Making your demands more adaptive and flexible will encourage you to progress.

Overgeneralisation

Overgeneralisation occurs when you take one situation and apply it to be something that would occur all the time. If you have arranged for a friend to help you with your de-cluttering and you receive a message that they are not able to meet you that day, you feel let down. You may have the opportunity to reorganise your friend's visit, but not when you jump to the conclusion that they will let you down again just because it has happened once before. Another example could be that you clear your space, gradually fill it with more items again and feel that because you have had one setback then nothing is ever going to change. This will lead you to feel demotivated and give up.

Blame, or personalisation:

When you feel that something is your fault you are personalising. For example, you may feel it is your fault that your space has become cluttered. Blame or personalisation is not helpful as it prevents you developing the compassionate understanding of your problem that would be more helpful.

Fortune telling

You may feel that you know how things are going to turn out. If you are getting a friend to help you with the de-cluttering, you predict that they are going to throw everything out and you will have no control. The result is that you experience negative emotions and feel that you are not able to cope, preventing you from doing the work you had intended to do. Fortune telling is forecasting how things are going to be without experience.

Low frustration tolerance

You hide from uncomfortable feelings when you have low frustration tolerance. For example, when de-cluttering you might experience negative feelings and, as a result, you avoid feeling this way by engaging with other activities that are not related to your hoarding. Or you might experience negative emotions when attempting to discard items you have saved and this could result in you continuing to save them as a way of coping with those feelings. Low frustration tolerance leads you to avoid engaging with your hoarding issues.

Unhelpful Thinking Patterns

Common distortions in thinking which help maintain emotional problems.

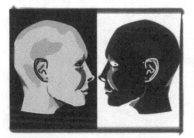

Black and white thinking

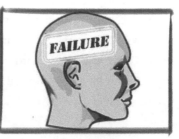

Labelling

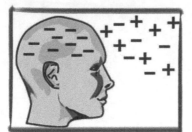

Mental filtering

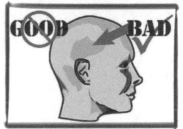

Disqualifying the positive

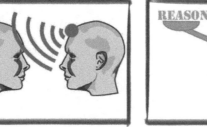

Mind reading

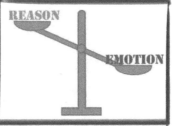

Emotional reasoning

Appendix

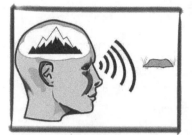

Catastrophising

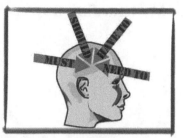

Demands

Over generalising

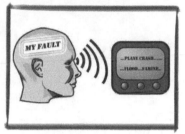

Blame/Personalisation

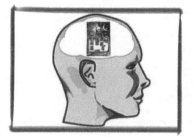

Fortune telling

Low frustration tolerance

My hoarding flower

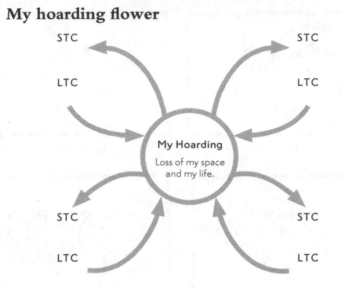

STC

LTC

STC

LTC

My Hoarding
Loss of my space
and my life.

STC

LTC

STC

LTC

My reclaiming flower

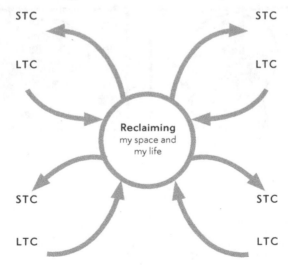

STC

LTC

STC

LTC

Reclaiming
my space and
my life

STC

LTC

STC

LTC

Cost/benefit analysis form

The benefits or advantages of:

....

....

....

....

....

....

....

....

....

....

....

....

....

....

....

....

....

Short term benefits

For myself   **For others**

....

....

....

....

....

....

....

....

....

....

....

....

....

....

....

....

....

Long term benefits

For myself   **For others**

....
....
....
....
....
....
....
....
....
....
....
....
....
....
....
....
....

Short term costs

For myself   **For others**

....

....

....

....

....

....

....

....

....

....

....

....

....

....

....

....

Long term costs

For myself	For others
....	....
....	....
....	....
....	....
....	....
....	....
....	....
....	....
....	....
....	....
....	....
....	....
....	....
....	....
....	....
....	....

Clutter Image Rating Scale

Frost, R.O., Steekee, G., Tolin, D, & Renaud, S. (2008). 'Development and validation of the clutter image rating.' *Journal of Psychopathology and Behavioural Assessment,* 30(3): 193–203.

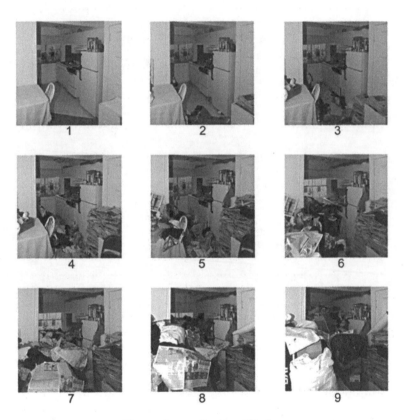

Clutter Image Rating: Kitchen

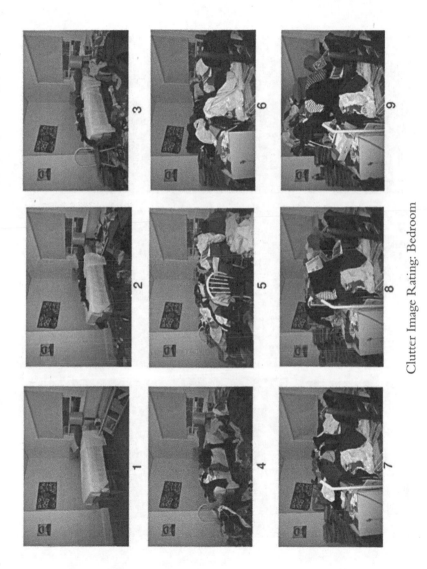

Clutter Image Rating: Bedroom

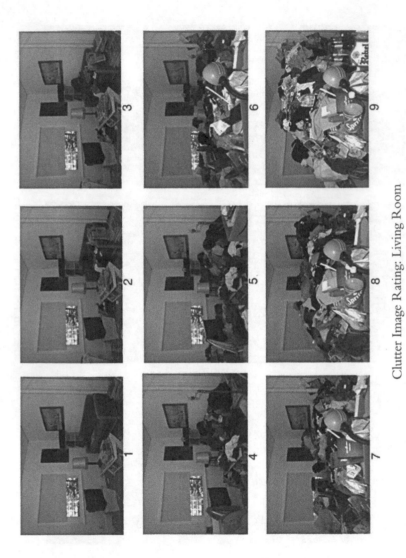

Clutter Image Rating: Living Room

Useful resources

UK

British Association for Behavioural and Cognitive
Psychotherapies
telephone: 0161 705 4304
web: www.babcp.com

British Psychological Society
telephone: 0116 254 9568
web: www.bps.org.uk

Hoarding UK
telephone: 020 3239 1600
web: www.hoardinguk.org

OCD Action
telephone: 0845 390 6232
web: www.ocdaction.org.uk

OCD UK
telephone: 0845 120 3778
web: www.ocduk.org

Europe

European Association for Behavioural and
Cognitive Therapy
telephone: +31 30 254 30 54
web: www.eabct.eu

USA

American Psychological Association
telephone: +1 800 374 2721 or +1 202 336 5500
web: www.apa.org

Anxiety and Depression Association of America
telephone: +1 240 485 1001
web: www.adaa.org

Association for Behavioral and Cognitive Therapies
telephone: +1 212 647 1890/1927/0019
web: www.abct.org

International OCD Foundation
telephone: +1 617 973 5801
web: iocdf.org

Canada

Canadian Association of Cognitive and Behavioural
Therapies (CACBT)
web: cacbt.ca/en/index.htm
eMentalHealth.ca
telephone: +1 613 738 6990
web: www.ementalhealth.ca/Canada/Hoarding/index.
php?m=article&ID=13330

Rest of the world

Asia

Asian Cognitive Behavioral Therapy Association
(ACBTA)
web: asiancbt.wccbly.com

Australia

Anxiety Recovery Centre Victoria
telephone: +61 1300 269 438
web: www.arcvic.org.au/
obsessive-compulsive-disorder/229

Anxiety Treatment Australia
telephone: +61 0419 104 284 or 03 9819 3671
web: www.anxietyaustralia.com.au/anxiety-help/
compulsive-hoarding/

Australian Association for Cognitive and Behaviour Therapy
web: www.aacbt.org

Catholic Community Services, Sydney
telephone: +61 1800 225 474
web: squalorandhoarding.catholiccommunityservices.com.au

New Zealand

AnzaCBT: Aotearoa New Zealand Association for Cognitive and Behavioural Therapies
web: www.cbt.org.nz

Engage Aotearoa
telephone: +64 9 963 9455
web: www.engagenz.co.nz

South Africa

Health 24
web: http://www.health24.com/Mental-Health/
Living-with-mental-illness/Extreme-hoarding-20120721

Bibliography

American Psychiatric Association, (2013). *Diagnostic and Statistical Manual 5*, New York: American Psychiatric Association

Singh, S. and Jones, C. (2012), 'Visual Research Methods: a novel approach to understanding the experiences of compulsive hoarders', *Journal of Cognitive and Behavioural Psychotherapy Research*, 1 (1), pp. 36–42

Steketee, G. and Frost R. O. (2014). *Treatment of Hoarding Disorder Workbook* (2nd Edition). New York: Oxford University Press (pp. 104–106)

Index

accountability, 37, 316–17
activities, engaging in, 297–308
adjustment disorders, 14
American Psychiatric
  Association, 8
anger, 12, 133, 184
anti-social behaviour orders
  (ASBOs), 13
anxiety, 12, 14, 15, 41, 88, 97,
  108, 112, 199–201
attention deficit hyperactivity
  disorder (ADHD), 14
avoidant behaviour, 88, 145–6,
  280–1, 285, 290, 294

bags
  colour and type of, 45
  and decision-making, 166
  and record-keeping, 40–1,
    266, 272, 283, 328
Beck, Aaron T., viii
behaviours, 21, 117–18, 145,
  172–3, 180, 238
  conceptualising, 86–95,
    317–18
  replacement, 121–6

see also avoidant behaviour;
  engaging behaviour
beliefs, 117–18, 145, 172, 199,
  238, 282
  conceptualising, 96–107, 317
  identifying, 97–107, 180–98
  replacement, 121–6
  and uncomfortable feelings,
    111–15
  and unhelpful thinking
    patterns, 184–9
bereavement disorder, 14
bills, 26, 166
black-and-white thinking, 184,
  201, 221, 330–1
blame, *see* personalisation

catastrophising, 186–7, 333
charity shops, 284, 323
churning, *see* internal recycling
clutter image rating scale,
  153–64, 266, 272, 281,
  344–6
Cognitive Behavioural Therapy
  (CBT), viii–x, 1–2, 21–3,
  145, 199

Index

Index

357